Palestinian Prisoners

Palestinian Prisoners

A Question of Conscience

Edited by
John Calhoun and Ranjan Solomon

This report on the state of Palestinian prisoners has been produced by the Palestine Israel Ecumenical Forum, in cooperation with
Addameer
Hurryyat
DCI—Palestine
Kairos Palestine
Jerusalem Inter Church Centre

For further information on these groups, see the listing in the back of this volume.

PALESTINIAN PRISONERS
A Question of Conscience

WCC Publications is the book publishing programme of the World Council of Churches. Founded in 1948, the WCC promotes Christian unity in faith, witness and service for a just and peaceful world. A global fellowship, the WCC brings together 345 Protestant, Orthodox, Anglican and other churches representing more than 560 million Christians in 110 countries and works cooperatively with the Roman Catholic Church.

Opinions expressed in WCC Publications are those of the authors.

Cover design: Linda Hanna
Cover image: A little girl stands in front of Ofer prison with a picture of Khader Adnan Mohamad Musa. Khader Adnan is a 36-year-old Palestinian who has spent most part of the last three years in prison under the dubious administrative detention act. He went on a 66-day hunger strike in protest of his administrative detention and the ill-treatment he suffered at the hands of the Israeli Prison Service, during which he ran the grave risk of death. He was released from prison on 17 April 2012 and began his slow recovery. He has since been rearrested in July 2014 and is currently being held in administrative detention once again. Khader Adnan is married with two daughters. His wife is pregnant with their third child. The story of Khader Adnan has been documented by Addameer, whose lawyers have followed up on his case on each occasion he was arrested.

Book design and typesetting: 4 Seasons Book Design / Michelle Cook
ISBN: 978-2-8254-1653-2

World Council of Churches
150 route de Ferney, P.O. Box 2100
1211 Geneva 2, Switzerland
www.oikoumene.org

Contents

Preface													vii

1. Palestinian Political Prisoners: An Overview						1

2. Administrative Detention in the Occupied
   Palestinian Territories											15

3. Ailing Prisoners in Israeli Occupation Jails						29

4. Families and Family Visits										57

5. Palestinian Children Detained in the Israeli Military
   Court System													69

6. Conscientious Objectors										93

7. Organizations Working with Prisoners
   and Human Rights											101

Preface

This resource book is published in conjunction with the World Week for Peace in Palestine Israel (WWPPI), an initiative of the Palestine Israel Ecumenical Forum of the World Council of Churches. It is based on the topic of Palestinian prisoners and the theme explored in the last year, "Let my people go." The choice of the theme clearly underscores the crisis that affects several thousand Palestinians and their families.

The Palestine Israel Ecumenical Forum views its focus on prisoners during the WWPPI as imperative due to the gravity of the situation. The conditions prevailing over the last few decades demand that churches join campaigns which insist on justice for the thousands who are wrongfully confined. These conditions were only exacerbated by the 2014 Israel-Gaza conflict.

The arbitrary detention of Palestinians, especially the use of "administrative detention" by Israeli occupation forces, has had a devastating effect on Palestinian society. Israel's use of mass detention and imprisonment of Palestinians as a policy aims to suppress any resistance to Israel's continued occupation, and also to delay the development of Palestinian social and political institutions. Nearly every family in Palestine has been directly or indirectly affected by Israel's policy of arbitrary and illegal detention. It is an issue that speaks to people's hearts in Palestine.

In 2007, at an international conference of church leaders held in Amman, Jordan, Christians from Gaza to Jerusalem to Nazareth called out with one voice to their brothers and sisters worldwide in Christ. Their urgent plea was clear: "Enough is enough. No more words without deeds. It is time for action." Today Palestinian Christians are once again calling on the international community to rise up with one voice to say no to the illegalities and discrimination inherent in Israel's policy and practice of detention.

Palestinians ask churches, civil society, academics, artists, and individuals worldwide to participate in activities of WWPPI; to campaign for the release of Palestinians unjustly detained; and to work for the deliverance of all who are bound by the shackles of conflict, violence, injustice, mistrust and prejudice. Now is the moment for those who seek a just peace in Palestine Israel to abandon apathy, accept the risks of mission, and act concretely for justice in our times!

The Palestine Israel Ecumenical Forum is grateful for the cooperation received from the following human rights organizations: Addameer, Hurryyat, DCI-Palestine, the Jerusalem Inter Church Centre, and New Profile. Their staff members have put in hour upon hour of work to offer the international community a comprehensive set of facts, testimonies, and analysis of the lives of Palestinian prisoners and their families. Most of the statistical and legal information in this publication comes from them. We are proud to publish this dossier with their cooperation.

It is our hope that participants in the World Week for Peace in Palestine Israel will experience close and transformative encounters with the dreadful reality faced by those living under occupation in Palestine. Working together across the religious divide in Palestine and Israel, and in unity with people who seek justice across the world, regardless of religion and ethnicity, we can help bring an end to the illegal occupation of Palestine. We can. We must.

John Calhoun
Moderator, International Working Group
World Week for Peace in Palestine Israel

Ranjan Solomon
PIEF Staff Coordinator
World Week for Peace in Palestine Israel

1. Palestinian Political Prisoners: An Overview

Since the Israeli occupation of Palestinian territories in 1967, Palestinians have been charged with offenses under Israeli military law and tried in military courts. Over the last 47 years, an estimated 750,000 Palestinians have been detained under Israeli military orders in the occupied Palestinian territory (OPT), which constitutes approximately 20 percent of the total Palestinian population in the OPT, and as much as 40 percent of the total male Palestinian population. While arrests can occur at any time and in any place, Palestinians are most commonly arrested at checkpoints, off the street, at border crossings and from homes in the middle of the night. Upon arrest, detainees are usually cuffed with plastic handcuffs and blindfolded. Once bound and blindfolded, the detainee may be kept waiting, standing or kneeling, for long periods of time before being thrown on the floor of a military jeep, sometimes face down, for transfer to an interrogation center. During the transfer, which can take up to several hours, Israeli soldiers often abuse detainees. Cases of beatings, kicking, insults, threats and deliberate humiliation are routinely reported. Palestinians detainees are typically not informed of the reason for their arrest, nor are they told where they will be taken. Most children are subjected to the same treatment.

As of 1 May 2012, there were 5,271 Palestinian prisoners in Israeli detention including:

- 192 administrative detainees
- 196 child detainees
- 11 Palestinian Legislative Council members
- 17 women
- 476 Palestinians serving life sentences in Israeli prisons
- 30 prisoners sentenced for more than 20 years
- 30 prisoners arrested before the signing of the Oslo agreements

All but one of the prisons where Israel detains Palestinian prisoners are located inside Israel, in direct contravention of Article 76 of the Fourth Geneva Convention, which states that an Occupying Power must detain residents of an occupied territory in prisons inside the occupied territory. In addition to illegality under international law, the practical consequence of this system is that many prisoners have difficulty meeting with Palestinian defense counsel and do not receive family visits, since their attorneys and relatives are denied permits to enter Israel on "security grounds."

Legal Systems and Place of Residence

As mentioned, as of 1 May 2012, there were approximately 5271 Palestinian political prisoners held in Israeli prisons. Addameer defines political prisoners as any Palestinian—resident of the West Bank, including East Jerusalem, the Gaza Strip, or Israel—arrested in relation to the occupation. Of these prisoners, 192 were administrative detainees, 17 were women, 196 were children, and 11 were members of the Palestinian Legislative Council. In terms of origin, 298 were from East Jerusalem, 90 were citizens of Israel, 377 were from the Gaza Strip and the remainder (4,406) from the West Bank.

These prisoners are arrested on the basis of different legal systems, depending on their residence, whether in the West Bank, East Jerusalem, Gaza Strip or Israel.

West Bank

In the West Bank, Israeli authorities carry out arrests and detentions of Palestinians by virtue of a system of military regulations in place since the beginning of the occupation, with over 2,500 military orders issued over the past 47 years. Currently, the Order Regarding Security Provisions [Consolidated Version] (Judea and Samaria) (No. 1651), which replaces 20 pre-existing military orders, provides the authority to arrest and prosecute Palestinians from the West Bank for so-called "security" offences. These offences include injury to persons; offences against the authorities of the "area" and against the public order; obstruction of judicial proceedings; offences regarding weapons and war equipment, property, espionage or contact with enemy or hostile organization; and a number of other issues. Furthermore, Order No. 101 regarding the Prohibition of Acts of Incitement and Hostile Propaganda, issued in August 1967, criminalizes a range of civic activities including organizing and participating in protests, assemblies or vigils; waving flags and other political symbols; printing and distributing political material. The order also deems any acts of influencing public opinion as prohibited "political incitement," and under the heading of "support to a hostile organization," prohibits any activity that demonstrates sympathy for an organization deemed illegal under military orders, be it chanting slogans or waving a flag or other political symbols. Military Order 101 also establishes a basis for censorship in the occupied West Bank by forbidding any individual to "print or publicize in the region any publication of notice, poster, photo, pamphlet or other document containing material having a political significance," except in cases where the military commander has granted a permit.

Despite living in the same territory, Jewish settlers illegally residing in the West Bank and Israeli citizens committing "offences" in the West Bank, such as participating in demonstrations against the Annexation Wall in Palestinian villages, are not subjected to this legislation, but rather to Israeli criminal law, applied extra-territorially. Under this separate and unequal legal regime, Palestinians are subjected to more severe detention and sentencing provisions than Jewish settlers and Israeli citizens, with little or no effective judicial oversight.

Due process

Under military order 1651, Palestinians can be held for four days after their arrest before seeing a judge. This detention can be renewed for a period of 60 days, which can be extended to 90 days, without any charges being brought. During this period, a Palestinian can also be denied access to a lawyer for a maximum of 60 days. In comparison, Israeli settlers or citizens arrested under Israeli criminal law for a criminal offense committed in the West Bank can only be held for 24 hours without appearing before a judge. After these 24 hours, detention can only be renewed for a maximum period of 30 days without any charges being brought. Israelis accused of a criminal offence can only be denied access to a lawyer for a maximum of 48 hours.

Under military order 1651, if a Palestinian is ordered detained until the end of the legal proceedings, this detention can last up to 1.5 years, which may then be extended by six-month periods with no maximum limitation.

Under Israeli criminal law, applicable to settlers residing in the West Bank and Israelis committing offenses in the West Bank, detention until the end of legal proceedings can only last up to nine months, whether for a criminal or security offense. This detention can then be extended "from time to time," but only for periods of three months.

In addition, there are differences in the way charges are filed under Israeli military and criminal law. Under criminal law, charge sheets must be very detailed, including specific dates, time and place for the alleged offences the defendant is accused of. Under military law, on the other hands, no such specifics are required, making it virtually impossible to prove the defendant's innocence.

Sentencing provisions

Military order 1651 provides for harsher sentencing provisions than Israeli criminal law. Murder, for example, is punishable with the death penalty under military order 1651, article 209, although in practice such sentences are commuted to life imprisonment. In Israeli criminal law, on the other hand, murder is punishable by life imprisonment. However, under Israeli criminal law, if an offense is punishable by life imprisonment, but that penalty is not mandatory, then the maximum term of imprisonment that can be imposed by a court is 20 years. No such provision exists in Israeli military law applicable to Palestinians.

Similarly, while manslaughter is punishable by life imprisonment under military order 1651, it is only punishable by 20 years' imprisonment in Israeli law. Carrying, holding and manufacturing weapons is punished by life imprisonment under Israeli military law, but under Israeli criminal law, the maximum penalty is 15 years' imprisonment. With regard to incitement, while this "offence" is punishable by 10 years' imprisonment under Israeli military law, it is only punishable by a maximum of five years' imprisonment under Israeli criminal law. Under military law, there is no maximum set penalty for membership of an illegal organization, with a military court decision instead setting a precedent that the minimum penalty is 24 months' imprisonment. In fact some Palestinians, such as Ahmad Sa'adat, have been sentenced to as much as 30 years' imprisonment on such charges. Under Israeli criminal law, the maximum penalty is one year.

In addition, under Israeli criminal law, a person cannot be held criminally responsible for attempting to commit an offence if through his/her own decision or remorse, he/she refrained from committing it. Again, no such provision exists in Israeli military law.

In practice, the differences in law produce much higher sentences for Palestinians committing similar or lesser crimes than Israelis. On 21 January 2011, Israeli settler Nahum Korman, who beat an 11-year-old Palestinian child, Helmi Shusha, to death, was sentenced to 6 months of community service. On the same day, Suad Ghazal, a 15-year-old Palestinian girl accused of attempting to stab an Israeli settler, was sentenced to 6.5 years in prison.

Administrative detention

Under both military order 1651 (applicable to Palestinians) and the Emergency Powers (Detention) Law of 1979 (applicable to Israeli citizens), administrative detention orders can be issued for a period of 1-6 months, with no limits set on the number of times this detention can be renewed. However, while Palestinians must be brought before a judge for review of the order only within eight days of arrest, Israeli citizens must be brought before a judge within 48 hours of arrest. Furthermore, Israeli citizens are entitled to periodic review of their detention every three months, but there is no such provision for Palestinians.

While administrative detention has been used both regularly and on a large scale against Palestinians, historically only approximately nine settlers have been placed in administrative detention. Some Palestinians have spent as many as six and a half consecutive years in this form of detention, while settlers are on average only detained for a few months, with the longest reported period being the administrative detention of Israeli settler Noam Federman for nine months in 2004. Federman's case was also particular in that he was placed in administrative detention until the end of legal proceedings against him after he was charged with involvement in a 2002 attempt to bomb a girls' school in East Jerusalem. Furthermore, in 2005, the Jerusalem Magistrate's Court ordered the Israeli state to pay Federman NIS 100,000 as compensation for wrongfully placing him in administrative detention. It was the first time such a former administrative detainee was compensated for his detention.

Definition of children

Under Israeli domestic law applicable to Israeli citizens, the age of majority is defined as 18 while up until very recently the age of majority of Palestinians under military order 1651 was 16. On 27 September, the Israeli military commander of the West Bank issued military order 1676 to raise the age of Palestinian majority in the military court system from 16 to 18. Despite this, however, the amendment states that minors over the age of 16 may still be held in detention with adults, a provision that does not exist in Israeli criminal law. Furthermore, while Israeli children have the right to have a parent present during interrogation, this right is not fully accorded to Palestinian children under military legislation. Although military order 1676 includes a requirement to immediately notify the child's parents upon his or her arrest and interrogation, it also gives interrogators many openings to avoid this requirement. Furthermore, the amendment requires interrogators to inform minors of their right to an attorney but states that they will only notify an attorney "whose particulars were provided by the minor."

In general, Israel's Youth Law, which applies to Israeli minors, has been amended over the years to incorporate the rules of international law concerning the treatment of juveniles in criminal matters and the obligations derived from these rules. These amendments emphasize options for the rehabilitation of juveniles, their rights as human beings, the rights of witnesses who are minors, and more fundamentally favor alternatives to arrest, which is viewed as an absolute last resort. In contrast, despite the creation of a military court to try Palestinian children separately from adults in 2009, military legislation has not been amended to correct many of the due process deficiencies relating to the arrest and prosecution of Palestinian children.

Military courts

Palestinians from the West Bank who are arrested by the Israeli military and charged with security violations (as defined by Israel) and other crimes are prosecuted by two Israeli military courts located in Ofer and Salem in the OPT. Not all Palestinians who are arrested are prosecuted in the military courts; some are released while others are administratively detained without trial. Of those who are charged, approximately 99 percent are convicted,[1] and of these convictions, the vast majority is the result of plea bargains.[2]

As an Occupying Power, Israel has the right under international humanitarian law to establish military courts in the OPT, but applicable international human rights and humanitarian law restricts the jurisdiction of such courts to violations of criminal security legislation. The jurisdiction of Israeli military courts, however, is far broader and includes offenses unrelated to such legislation. Moreover, it is questionable whether the use of military courts to try civilians can ever satisfy the requirements under international human rights law that trials take place before independent and impartial tribunals. International law also guarantees certain fundamental fair trial rights, but these are regularly flouted by Israeli military courts:

The right to prompt notice of criminal charges: Israeli military orders contain no requirements that the charge be given to the accused without delay, and in a language he or she understands in, as required by international law. In practice, information on charges against the accused are often not disclosed by the prosecution until the day of the first hearing, which typically determines whether the accused will remain in detention until the end of the proceedings.

The right to prepare an effective defense: During interrogation, a detainee can be held for up to 60 days without access to a lawyer. Lawyers acting as defense counsel before the military courts highlight many further obstacles preventing an effective defense, including difficulties in meeting with their clients in detention facilities inside Israel, the lack of proper facilities to hold confidential meetings, court documents written in Hebrew, and the provision of incomplete prosecution material.

The right to trial without undue delay: Palestinians can be held in custody for four days before being brought before a judge. Furthermore, a Palestinian can be held without a charge for interrogation purposes, by order of a military judge, for an initial period of up to 60 days, which can be extended

---

1. Official Report of the Work of the Military Courts in the West Bank, 2010 (Hebrew) (Military Courts Report 2010).

2. See *infra*. Of the 8,516 cases concluded in the military courts in 2010, full evidentiary trials (in which witnesses were questioned, evidence was examined and closing statements were delivered) were conducted in only 82 – or 0.96 percent – of them.

for another period of up to 30 days. They can therefore be held for a total of 90 days before being charged.

The right to interpretation and translation: Israeli jurisprudence provides that a prisoner must be interrogated in his native language and that his statement also be written in that language, but in practice the detainee's confession or statement is frequently written in Hebrew, requiring the detainee to sign a statement he or she cannot understand. Moreover, all proceedings in the military courts are conducted in Hebrew with insufficient or inadequate translation.

The right to presumption of innocence: Israeli military orders do not include an explicit provision regarding the presumption of innocence. The exceedingly low rate of acquittals in the military courts, the practice of denying bail to the vast majority of pre-trial detainees, and the uncorrected prosecutorial reversal of the burden of proof against the accused all serve to indicate a strong presumption of guilt built into the military court system.

East Jerusalem

In East Jerusalem, although Israel imposed Israeli civil law upon its illegal annexation of the city in 1967, Palestinian residents continue to be subjected to a dual system of law: Israeli civil law and Israeli military regulations. In that framework, Israeli authorities often detain and interrogate Palestinians from East Jerusalem under military orders, a system that permits longer periods of detention, before transferring them to the Israeli civil system for trial, where prosecutors can seek higher sentences based on the principle that security offences are less common than in the military system in the OPT. The arrest and detention of Jewish settlers residing in East Jerusalem, however, is governed solely by Israeli civil law, which affords them greater protection and due process rights.

Gaza Strip

Before Israel's unilateral "withdrawal" from the Gaza Strip in 2005, a system of military orders similar to the one currently in place in the West Bank governed the arrest of Gazans. Since then, however, Gazans have been subjected to a different legal regime than Palestinians in the West Bank and are instead either arrested on the basis of Israeli criminal law, under which they are automatically classified as "security" prisoners and suffer from harsher standards of detention and sentencing than their Israeli "criminal" counterparts, or under the Incarceration of Unlawful Combatants Law.

In 2002, the Israeli Knesset passed the Incarceration of Unlawful Combatants Law, which is used to detain residents of the Gaza Strip without trial. Under this law, Israeli officers are authorized to order the internment of a Palestinian first for a period of 96 hours, which can then be renewed for an indefinite period of time, as opposed to administrative detention of Palestinians from the West Bank and Israeli citizens, which can only be ordered for a maximum of six months at a time. The internment can only be ended when one of the conditions for the internment ceases to exist or other reasons to justify the person's release arise. Alleged unlawful combatants must be brought before a judge within 14 days of the issuance of the internment order. If the order is confirmed by the judge, the internment must be reviewed every six months.

Detention conditions

Palestinians from the Gaza Strip detained in Israeli prisons have been subjected to additional discriminatory treatment as a result of Israel's June 2007 imposition of a total prohibition on family visits to these prisoners. On 9 December 2009, the Israeli High Court of Justice ruled against two petitions filed in 2008 by Palestinian and Israeli human rights organizations protesting the legality of the ban on family visits. The court held that the right to family visits in prison is not within the "framework of the basic humanitarian needs of the residents of the Strip, which Israel is obligated to enable." However, since the end of the mass hunger strike of 2012, family visits for Gaza prisoners have recommenced, although only every two months, as opposed to every two weeks for prisoners from the West Bank and Israel proper. In addition, starting in November 2009, Israel has effectively prevented these prisoners from receiving money from their families to buy basic necessities through the prison canteens by requiring that transfers of money be conditional on the physical presence of a family member at an Israeli bank—an impossibility for families residing in the Gaza Strip.

Israel

Finally, within the domestic criminal justice system itself, Israeli authorities discriminate between incarcerated Jewish and Palestinian citizens by distinguishing between criminal and "security" prisoners, with the majority of the latter being Palestinians. As of 1 December 2013, there were 5,060 security and 12,353 criminal prisoners in Israeli prisons. The overwhelming majority of these security prisoners were Palestinians from the West Bank, including East Jerusalem, and the Gaza Strip. Of the remaining security prisoners, the majority were Palestinians with Israeli citizenship. Although the exact numbers were not available for 2014, statistics from 2009 can also be used to illustrate the proportion of Jewish and Palestinian security prisoners. According to Adalah, in 2009 only 16 of the 7,740 security prisoners were Jewish.

Due process

Israeli citizens accused of committing a "security" offence may be held for four days before being brought before a judge. This detention can be renewed for a maximum period of 60 days without any charges being brought. During this period, the detainee can also be denied access to a lawyer for a maximum of 21 days. In comparison, Israeli citizens accused of committing a criminal offence can only be held for 24 hours without appearing before a judge. After these 24 hours, detention can only be renewed for a maximum period of 30 days without any charges being brought. Israelis accused of a criminal offense can only be denied access to a lawyer for a maximum of 48 hours.

Detention Facts and Figures

- 750,000 Palestinians arrested since 1967
- 50,000 arrested since the beginning of the Al-Aqsa Intifada
- 2,000 cases of torture in 2008 alone
- More than 600 complaints of torture and ill-treatment submitted against ISA interrogators since 2001
- Not one criminal investigation initiated
- Between March 2002 and October 2002, 15,000 Palestinians arrested in mass arrest campaigns

Treatment and Detention Conditions of Palestinian Political Prisoners

Palestinian political prisoners, whether from the West Bank, including East Jerusalem, the Gaza Strip, or Israel, are defined as "security" prisoners by Israel. As a result they are subjected to harsher interrogation techniques and more severe detention conditions than their Israeli criminal counterparts.

Interrogation, Torture and Ill-Treatment

As previously mentioned, under Israeli military orders, a Palestinian detainee can be interrogated for a total period of 90 days, during which he/she can also be denied lawyer visits for a period of 60 days.[3] During the interrogation period, a detainee is often subjected to some form of cruel, inhuman or degrading treatment, whether physical or psychological, and ranging in extremity.

The forms of torture and ill treatment employed against Palestinian prisoners include the following: beatings, tying prisoners in "stress positions," interrogation sessions that last up to 12 consecutive hours, depriving prisoners of sleep and other sensory deprivation, isolation and solitary confinement, and threats against the lives of their relatives. In past instances, detainees have died while in custody as a result of torture. Confessions extracted through such practices are admissible in court. Israel defends its interrogation techniques as a legitimate way of combating terrorism faced by its citizens, but in reality these practices are in direct contravention of international law, including the United Nations Convention against Torture (CAT), ratified by Israel on 3 October 1991, which requires any State Party to prevent the use of torture and associated practices.[4] The prohibition is absolute and non-derogable, and allows for "no exceptional circumstances whatsoever."[5]

On 6 September 1999, the Israeli High Court of Justice banned the use of torture during interrogation. A seemingly considerable victory for human

---

3. Previously, a Palestinian detainee could be interrogated for a total period of 188 days and denied lawyer visits for 90 days. This military order was amended to reflect the new interrogation periods on 1 August 2012.
4. Article 2(1) of the United Nations Convention Against Torture
5. Article 2(2) of the United Nations Convention Against Torture

rights defenders has proved in practice not to be applicable to Palestinian "security" detainees. Indeed, the ruling failed to explicitly forbid the use of torture but rather allowed that interrogation methods such as "moderate physical pressure"—widely deemed as torture—be used in situations where a detainee is considered a "ticking bomb." Furthermore, the ruling, while banning the use of the "necessity of defense" ex ante, continued to allow this defense post-factum in cases of "ticking bombs," thereby effectively allowing for impunity in cases of torture. As it stands in 2013, the use of torture and ill-treatment against Palestinian prisoners by Israeli authorities is so widespread to be rightly characterized as systematic. Since 1967, 72 prisoners have died as a result of torture.

Security prisoners are interrogated by the Israeli Security Agency (ISA), which often uses methods that amount to ill-treatment and torture. Criminal prisoners, on the other hand, are interrogated by the Israeli police, whose methods of operation are governed by a different set of rules. This has created two distinct regimes of interrogation, with the one affording less protection and rife with abuse used almost exclusively against Palestinians, whether from the OPT or Israel.

The use of physical pressure against prisoners and detainees is less common since the 1999 High Court ruling in *The Public Committee against Torture in Israel v. Government of Israel*, which placed certain restrictions on the use of torture during interrogation. However, as previously mentioned, under the court's decision, "moderate physical pressure" was allowed to continue in "necessity of defense" and in "ticking time-bomb" cases. As a result, Israeli interrogators continue to use forbidden interrogation techniques.

When complaints are filed against an ISA officer, they are submitted to the Attorney General, who decides whether to forward them to the Police Investigation Department (PID), an external body part of the Ministry of Justice, for criminal investigation. In practice, however, complaints are forwarded to the Officer in Charge of GSS Interrogee Complaints (OCGIC), an ISA officer, who reviews the complaint and is required to report directly to the Attorney General on the validity of the complaint. As a result, the OCGIC is thus responsible for investigating both his ISA colleagues and the detainee who registered the complaint. The conflict of interest in this matter is clear and undermines a detainee's right to an independent and impartial investigation. The results of this flawed structure are clear: according to the Public Committee against Torture in Israel (PCATI), the recourse to PID has not been used once in recent years. In addition, all torture allegations and complaints are either denied or justified under the banner of "necessity defense," and none of the 621 complaints submitted between September 2001 and September 2009 resulted in a criminal investigation. In a few isolated cases, disciplinary measures have been applied against ISA officers, but none included harsh measures such as fines, dismissal or demotion.

Detention Conditions

Detention conditions differ greatly between criminal and "security" prisoners. Privileges such as the ability to make phone calls, receive family visits without a glass divider, and make occasional visits outside the prison are only available to criminal prisoners. Indeed, while criminal prisoners may use phones on a regular basis, "security" prisoners are denied the use of phones, except in exceptional circumstances, such as the death of a family member; but even then, authorization must be obtained from prison officials. Security prisoners are confined to their cells for the majority of the day, except for a few hours of recreation. No such restrictions are imposed on criminal prisoners. Discrimination is especially apparent in education, with criminal prisoners enjoying rich and well-organized formal and informal education programs while "security" prisoners, including minors, are entitled only to minimal education programs. Adult "security" prisoners, for example, can only study by correspondence at the Open University, which only offers studies in Hebrew. While criminal prisoners may be eligible for occasional visits outside of prison, this is virtually impossible for Palestinian "security" prisoners. In addition, other rights, such as the right to be released on parole, are applied preferentially to criminal prisoners, with only a very small percentage of security prisoners eligible for early release.

In practice, Israel also discriminates between Jewish and Palestinian "security" prisoners by offering preferential treatment to the former. Ami Popper, a former Israeli army officer, was sentenced to seven life sentences for killing seven Palestinians in 1990, although his sentence was commuted to 40 years in 1999. During his imprisonment, Popper, who is categorized as a "security" prisoner, has married and fathered three children. He has also been able to take hundreds of vacations outside prison, during one of which, while driving without a valid license, he was involved in a car accident that killed his first wife and one of his children.

Conclusion

It is quite clear that Israel is using the mass detention and imprisonment of Palestinians as a policy. This policy has the dual objective of suppressing any resistance to Israel's continued occupation and colonization, while at the same time preventing from any sort of normal Palestinian society from emerging. Given the fact that most Palestinian families living in the OPT have suffered in some form or another from this policy, the issue of the prisoners is very close to peoples heart in Palestine.

Israel continues to target the student, community and political leadership of Palestinian society and subjects them to a wide range of grave violations on a daily basis - from the moment of arrest, through interrogation, and eventual imprisonment. The treatment of Palestinians, however, is in stark contrast to that of Jewish Israelis.

Israel's arrest and detention of Palestinians in the OPT and within Israel proper is governed by a regime of laws and institutions almost completely separate from the one administering the arrest of Jewish Israelis. Because this system enables the large-scale arbitrary arrest of Palestinians while generally affording them lower protections and guarantees than Jewish Israelis, it should be understood as a discriminatory institutional tool of domination and oppression against them.

2. Administrative Detention in the Occupied Palestinian Territories

Administrative detention is a procedure under which detainees are held without a charge or trial. No charges are filed, and there is no intention of bringing the detainee to trial. In accordance with the detention order, a detainee is given a specific term of detention. On or before the expiry of the term, the detention order is frequently renewed. This process can be continued indefinitely.

Administrative detention has been commonly used by repressive regimes to circumvent the legal process and to hinder access by political dissidents to the protection that they should be entitled to under the law. Places where it has been used to a particular extent include Northern Ireland, South Africa (under apartheid), the United States, and Israel.

The possibility of becoming an administrative detainee is an ever-present threat in the daily lives of all Palestinians and severely impacts the lives of Palestinians living in the occupied Palestinian territory. Over the years, Israel has held Palestinians in prolonged detention without trying them or informing them of the suspicions against them. While detainees may appeal the detention, neither they nor their attorneys are allowed to see the evidence. Israel has therefore made a mockery out of the entire system of procedural safeguards in both domestic and international law regarding the right to freedom.

Administrative detention in the OPT is ordered by a military commander and grounded on "security reasons." Detainees are held without trial and without being told the evidence against them. In most cases, they are simply informed that there is "secret evidence" against them and that they are being held for security reasons.

The security reasons are broad enough to include peaceful political subversion and virtually any act of resistance against the Israeli colonial occupation. The definitions of crimes in Israeli legislation are additional sites where ambiguity can be manipulated, often resulting in increased sentences and imprisonment for Palestinians. For example, participation in a demonstration is deemed a disruption of public order. Firing in the air during a wedding, as a form of celebration, constitutes a danger to Israel's national security, despite the fact that it occurs in areas ostensibly under the sole jurisdiction of the Palestinian Authority (Area A).

Carrying or placing a Palestinian flag is a crime under Israeli military regulations. Even pouring coffee for a member of a declared illegal association can be seen as support for a terrorist organization. Palestinian national security forces are also seen as an illegal association.

Administrative Detention in Numbers

During the period from March 2002 to October 2002, Israeli Occupation Forces (IOF) arrested over 15,000 Palestinians during mass arrest campaigns, rounding up males in cities and villages between the ages of 15 to 45. In October 2002, there were over 1,050 Palestinians in administrative detention. By the beginning of March 2003, Israel held more than one thousand Palestinians in administrative detention.

In 2007, Israel held a monthly average of 830 administrative detainees, which was one hundred higher than in 2006. Furthermore, during the Palestinian Legislative Council (PLC) elections of 2006, Israel placed dozens of candidates from the Islamic "Change and Reform Party" in administrative detention, some of whom are still imprisoned to this day. Over the years, only nine Israeli citizens from illegal settlements in the West Bank have reportedly been detained for periods up to six months.

On 17 April 2012, approximately 1,200 Palestinian prisoners started hunger strikes and an additional 2,300 refused meals from the IPS in protest of prison conditions, administrative detention and restrictions on family visitation. After 28 days of hunger strike, the prisoners were able to strike an agreement with the IPS that ended the strike, including a provision that new administrative detention orders or renewals of administrative detention orders for the Palestinians currently in administrative detention would be limited, unless the secret files, upon which the administrative detention is based, contained "very serious" information. However, the Israeli security forces reneged on their agreement to release administrative detainees who were on hunger strike, causing several to go on individual hunger strikes, including Thaer Halahleh, Bilal Diab and Akram Rikhawi.

In response to Israel's failure to honor the agreement and its continued use of administrative detention, approximately 100 administrative detainees launched a mass hunger strike on 24 April 2014. Israel responded with a number of punitive measures, including the immediate isolation of the hunger strikers from the rest of the prison population; the transfer of hunger strikers to different prisons; the isolation of the strikers' leadership; the restriction of access to legal counsel; the denial of family visits for periods of four to six months; daily violent searches; beatings; the denial of salt; and confiscation of all personal belongings.

As the days passed, the hunger strikes escalated as more administrative detainees and prisoners joined the strike. On 8 June 2013 it became the longest mass hunger strike in Palestinian history as the hunger strikers had gone 46 days without food. The strike ended on 27 June.

As of 1 May 2014 there were 192 administrative detainees in Israeli prisons and detention centers, including 8 members of the Palestinian Legislative Council.

Administrative Detention: A Legal Perspective

International humanitarian law, comprised primarily of the Geneva Conventions of 1949 and their Additional Protocols, as well as international human rights law, provide the international legal standards that are to be applied to administrative detention in armed conflict and other situations of violence. International law permits administrative detention under specific, narrowly defined circumstances.

In accordance with the International Covenant on Civil and Political Rights (ICCPR), there must be a public emergency that threatens the life of the nation. Furthermore, administrative detention can only be ordered on an individual case-by-case basis, without discrimination of any kind. A

Ahmad Rimawi: The Youngest Administrative Detainee on Hunger Strike

Name: Ahmad Ishraq Irhemi Rimawi
Date of Arrest: 17 November 2012
Date of Birth: 12 November 1994
Residence: Abwein, Ramallah
Occupation: Student
Prison: Negev "Naqab" prison
Legal Status: Administrative Detainee
Number of AD Orders: 3

Days after his 18th birthday, Ahmad and two friends were travelling through 'Atara checkpoint on the night of 17 November 2012 when they were stopped by Israeli Occupation Forces (IOF) and their taxi searched. Ahmad was arrested, transferred to Ofer Prison and had an administrative detention order issued against him on 20 November, which has subsequently been renewed multiple times.

Both of his friends were also arrested at the checkpoint on 17 November 2012. One of them, a US citizen of Palestinian descent, was deported to the United States. The other, a US citizen and West Bank resident, was released on bail after a few days in detention.

Prison reunites Ahmad and his father

Ahmad Rimawi's family has been plagued by the Occupation's detention policies since 2001, when Ishraq, his father, was arrested on 15 June 2001 and sentenced to nineteen years. Shortly after the arrest, the family home in Beit Reema was demolished, and the entire extended family of twenty was forced to live in a tent for one month before moving into a relative's home in the nearby village of Abwein. Ahmad's mother is the only provider for the family, causing extreme hardship. Ahmad also has two younger sisters.

Since the age of seven, Ahmad only knows his father behind the glass divider that stands between them during the bi-monthly family visits. Families suffer greatly from their treatment for family visits, many of them denied permits for "security reasons," keeping them estranged from their loved ones for years at a time. For Ahmad, it wasn't until his arrest that he was reunited with his father in Ofer prison.

However, Ahmad was transferred to the Negev prison in an attempt to keep the father and son separated. Ishraq submitted several requests to be transferred to the Negev prison with his son, which were routinely denied until early 2014. Now, after thirteen years of separation, Ahmad and his father are detained in the same prison cell. Um Ahmad has lamented the bittersweet nature of her husband and son's detentions saying, "Despite the cruelty of prison and detention, I am somewhat reassured that my son is with his father; being together might actually make the cruel conditions of detention a little easier on them."

The conditions in the Negev prison are harsh on both the prisoners and their families. Prisoners complain of the stifling heat, insects and poor living conditions. Family visits are only allowed once a month, while in other prisons, visitation rights are twice a month.

Administrative detention

Upon Ahmad's arrest, he was interrogated for two days and accused of participating in "military activities," all accusations that he denied. His first administrative detention order was issued on 20 November 2012 for six months. His order has been renewed three consecutive times, with the most recent order expiring on 15 May 2014.

All appeals submitted to the Military Court have been rejected thus far. Addameer lawyer Aouda Zbeidat has also filed an appeal to the High Court, which has also been rejected. The consistent rejections to the appeals suggest that Ahmad might have his administrative detention renewed again.

The courts have refused to take into account Ahmad's age, or the fact that his administrative detention is preventing him from continuing his education. In the latest appeal hearing, the Military Judge stated, "The fact that the detainee is child does not make him immune to detention."

Hunger strike

On 24 April 2014 Ahmed, along with approximately 100 other administrative detainees, launched a mass hunger strike in protest of the continued administrative detention. To date he has gone 46 days without food, with no end to the strike in sight.

No charges, no evidence

Ahmad's case presents a clear example of how administrative detention orders are renewed based solely on decisions by the Israeli intelligence, not the Military Court. According to Israeli Military Law, the General Security Services (Shabak) issue the administrative detention orders, which the military commander of the region signs. The order is then presented to a Military Judge for a final review, accompanied with a "secret" file that includes the recommendations from the intelligence. This secret file cannot be viewed by the detainee or his lawyer. In most cases, the administrative detention order is approved by the judge during a secret session in the absence of the detainee or his lawyer, making it virtually impossible for an intervention on behalf of the detainee.

These practices confirm the impunity by which the Israeli intelligence functions and also the complicity and collaboration between the Israeli military court judge, prosecution and intelligence. These practices bring into question the validity of the military courts due to their lack of accountability or fair trials.

Ahmad's case file includes only a speculation of his alleged "offenses," without providing any evidence or data against him. The intelligence has not provided any new information, evidence or materials for the renewal of his administrative detention orders.

In the renewal hearings, the military judge did not request documentation to support the military prosecution's recommendations to renew his administrative detention. The judge also did not request a list of charges or accusations to allow Ahmad's lawyer to prepare an appropriate defense or appeal. Ahmad's case is not unique in that virtually all administrative detention orders are renewed without further investigation into the case, or based on old information.

Article (9) of the International Covenant on Civil and Political Rights states that "everyone has the right to liberty and security of person. No one shall be subjected to arbitrary arrest or detention." And Article (78) of the Fourth Geneva Convention states that administrative detention shall be practiced only for imperative reasons of security.

Administrative detention violates the Fourth Geneva Convention. It also constitutes a form of torture within a systematic policy which is a violation of the Fourth Geneva Convention and amounts to a war crime and a crime against humanity.

state's collective, non-individual detention of a whole category of persons can in no way be considered a proportional response, regardless of what the circumstances of the emergency concerned might be.

According to Adalah, the Legal Center for Arab Minority Rights in Israel, Israel has sought to justify its policy of administrative detention by the remarkable claim that it has been under a "state of emergency since 1948" and is therefore justified in suspending or derogating "from certain rights, including the right not to be arbitrarily detained." Moreover, administrative detention should not be used as a substitute for criminal prosecution where there is insufficient evidence to obtain a conviction. Israel's use of administrative detention deliberately infringes these restrictions.

International Law

In 1967, Israel occupied the West Bank, including East Jerusalem (both were under Jordanian control at the time) and the Gaza Strip (which was under Egyptian administration), which have come to be known as the OPT. Israel also occupied the Golan Heights and the Sinai Peninsula at the same time. Israel thus became a "belligerent power" and subject to international humanitarian law in regard to the occupation of these territories.

Humanitarian law regulates how such territories should be governed, the conduct of the occupying power, and the treatment of the civilian population ("protected persons") during occupation. The key international humanitarian legal instruments that regulate administrative detention in the occupied Palestinian territory are:

- The Fourth Geneva Convention (1949)
- Additional Protocol I to the Geneva Convention (1977)
- Regulations Annexed to the Hague Convention No. IV
  (Hague Regulations)

An international consensus exists among States and the International Committee of the Red Cross (ICRC) that the Fourth Geneva Convention and the Hague Regulations of 1907 apply to all of the territories occupied by Israel after the 1967 war. The United Nations Security Council and the International Court of Justice (ICJ) have confirmed the applicability of the is no limit on the amount of times an administrative detention order can be extended. This in effect allows for indefinite arbitrary detention.

In June 1999, the procedure governing administrative detention orders was modified by Military Order 1466, which provided that a detainee must be brought before a military judge within ten days of his or her arrest. These modifications also authorized the military judge to approve administrative detention orders as issued, cancel them altogether or decrease the duration of the order. In March 2002, during the Second Intifada, another amendment was issued, extending the period a detainee can be held without seeing a judge to 18 days. By the end of 2002, the limit returned to eight days, but ISA representatives were no longer required to come to court and present the secret evidence. Military Order 1651, which currently authorizes administrative detention, reduced the period of time an administrative detainee can be held without seeing a judge to four days, though a temporary order included in Order 1651 (Chapter I, Article B) currently allows a detainee to be prevented from seeing a judge for eight days (Chapter I, Article B 287).

The Law in the Gaza Strip

Until the Israeli military's withdrawal from the Gaza Strip in 2005, administrative detention was authorized in Gaza under Military Order 941 (1988) and was similar in its operation to the administrative detention order in operation in the West Bank. After the withdrawal, the Israeli government argued that it is no longer an Occupying Power in the Gaza Strip and that it is not bound by international law relating to the duties and obligations of occupying powers. There is consensus among the international community, however, that despite the withdrawal of Israeli military troops in 2005, there are ongoing as well as new methods of Israeli military and administrative control in the Gaza Strip, which amount to "effectual control" of the area. Therefore, the withdrawal of Israeli troops alone does not mean that Gaza is no longer occupied by Israel. It is important to note that facts on the ground define the legal situation. Israel maintains its effective control over the Gaza Strip by different means, such as control over air space, sea space and international borders. Israel also continues to exercise control, although indirectly, over Palestinian movement in the Rafah crossing – the only exit outside of Gaza to countries other than Israel – namely Egypt. Furthermore,

Israel continues to exercise control over the movement of Palestinians, as well as goods, in the Kerem Shalom, Erez, Karni, and Sufa crossings. Even during the period between the Israeli withdrawal in September 2005 and the Israeli military operation dubbed "Operation Summer Rains" in 2006, there has been a consensus among the international community that Israel, regardless of the applicability of the laws of occupation, continues to be legally responsible for protected persons that live in the Gaza Strip under general provisions of international humanitarian law.

In March 2002, the Knesset enacted the Incarceration of Unlawful Combatants Law. This law provides for the indefinite administrative detention of foreign nationals and creates a third category of person: the unlawful combatant "with an unclear definition that includes not only persons who participate in hostilities" against Israel, but also any members of forces that carry out such hostilities of that force. The usage of the "unlawful combatant" designation runs contrary to the distinction in international humanitarian law between combatants and civilians. It affords detainees neither the protection of the Third Geneva Convention as combatants held as prisoners of war, nor the protection of the Fourth Geneva Convention as civilians. Neither of these conventions prevents the state from prosecuting suspects for crimes they allegedly committed either as combatants or civilians.

Israel's Position toward International Law

Although Israel has stated that it generally applies the humanitarian provisions of the Fourth Geneva Convention in the Occupied Territory (without specifying exactly which provisions it is referring to—a de facto application), it denies that it is legally obliged to do so (a de jure application). Israel bases this argument on a narrow interpretation of Article 2 of the Convention. Israel argues that the Convention only applies between two High Contracting Parties, one of which has sovereignty over the territory occupied by the other. Israel posits that Jordan and Egypt were not acting as sovereigns over the Occupied Territory prior to 1967 (being more in the position of administrators) and that there is no other relevant High Contracting Party, therefore the Convention does not apply.

The ICJ rejected this argument, noting that both Jordan and Egypt were High Contracting Parties to the Covenant in 1967 and that Article 2 does not impose any qualification of sovereignty when referring to the territory of a High Contracting Party.

Israel's argument also ignores Article 4 of the Convention, which is intended to protect the rights of people who find themselves "in the hands of a Party to the conflict or occupying Power of which they are not nationals," regardless of the competing claims to sovereignty over the territory. Rejecting Israel's argument, the ICJ concluded that,

This interpretation reflects the intention of the drafters of the Fourth Geneva Convention to protect civilians who find themselves, in whatever way, in the hands of the occupying Power. Whilst the drafters of the Hague Regulations of 1907 were as much concerned with protecting the rights of a State whose territory is occupied, as with protecting the inhabitants of that territory, the drafters of the Fourth Geneva Convention sought to guarantee the protection of civilians in time of war, regardless of the status of the occupied territories, as is shown by Article 47 of the Convention.

Finally, the ICJ noted that the Israeli Supreme Court has itself acknowledged the application of the Convention in relation to military action undertaken by the IOF in the Rafah refugee camp in the Gaza Strip.

Administrative Detention in Practice

Administrative detention orders in the occupied Palestinian territory are issued by military commanders for a period of time between one to six months and can be renewed indefinitely.

Procedure

Under Israeli military regulations the system of administrative detention is implemented as follows:

1. Palestinians are usually arrested by the Israeli military. Large numbers of Israeli soldiers often forcibly enter the home for an arrest, usually breaking down doors and destroying personal property. Arrests also commonly take place at checkpoints and at demonstrations. In some cases, police dogs are used to enter the home, terrifying the occupants. Soldiers also verbally and physically threaten the occupants of the house.

2. A Palestinian can then be detained for up to eight days without being informed of the reason for his or her detention and without being brought before a judge. Between April and June 2002, during Israel's mass arrest campaign in the OPT, this period of time was increased by the Israeli Military Order 1500 to 18 days. This is in breach of international law.

3. During or following the eight days of detention, a detainee is either (a) sent to an interrogation center, (b) charged with an offense, (c) given an administrative detention order, or (d) released.

4. Once an administrative detention order has been issued by the military commander, the detainee must be brought before a judge for a judicial review within eight days. Occasionally, the matter will be dealt with at the first hearing and the order approved or varied.

5. At the judicial review, secret evidence is submitted by the Israeli Security Agency (ISA). Neither the detainee nor his or her lawyer is permitted to see the secret evidence. This is in breach of international law.

6. The hearing is not open to the public. This is in breach of international law.

7. The military judge may approve, shorten or cancel the order. In practice, the order is usually approved without change.

8. Previously, administrative detention orders had to be reviewed after three months. However, in April 2002, this requirement was abolished. Upon the initial judgment, the case can be appealed to the Military Court of Appeals, and then, if necessary to the Israeli High Court of Justice.

9. At the end of the initial detention period the order can be renewed for another period of up to six months. There is no limitation on the number of times the initial detention period can be renewed. Each time an administrative detention order is renewed the detainee is given a new "hearing."

As a result of the possibility of indefinite renewal of administrative detention orders, detainees do not know when they will be released and/or why they are being detained. In some cases, administrative detention orders are renewed at the prison's gate. In many of the legal cases pursued by Addameer, administrative detainees spent years in prison after being sentenced for committing violations, in accordance with military orders. When the period ended, however, rather than being released they were placed under administrative detention under the pretext that they still posed a threat to "security." Palestinian detainees have spent up to eight years in prison without a charge or trial under administrative detention orders.

Lawyers

Lawyers who represent Palestinians in Israeli military and civil courts face obstacles that systematically erode the right of Palestinian detainees to legal representation. Defense attorneys must contend with military orders, Israeli laws and prison procedures that curtail their ability to provide adequate counsel to their clients. A lawyer's citizenship or residency status dictates his or her ability to represent Palestinian clients. This is a breach of international law.

The military prosecutor is usually the only source of information about the evidence in administrative detention cases; however, the defense lawyer cannot cross-examine the prosecutor as a witness. Instead, the prosecutor answers all of the defense lawyer's questions without being sworn in and has the right not to answer questions. A typical examination during a hearing to extend an administrative detention order goes as follows:

Q. Is any of the evidence open?
A. No.
Q. What is my client accused of?
A. Activities to help terrorism.
Q. How did he help terrorism?
A. He's in an organization.
Q. Which organization?
A. That is part of the secret evidence.
Q. Who else is in the organization with him?
A. That is part of the secret evidence.

It is rare for the defense to call witnesses as the evidence against the detainee is not known. In the circumstances, the only evidence that the defense can use is the good character of the detainee and his or her family life.

Conclusion

Addameer Prisoner Support and Human Rights Association contends that the practice of administrative detention in Israel and the occupied Palestinian territory contravenes fundamental human rights. Israel uses administrative detention in a highly arbitrary manner without putting even the most basic safeguards in place, leading to other, grave human rights violations, such as inhuman and degrading treatment and torture.

Addameer accordingly demands that all administrative detainees held on account of their political views or their activities carried out in resistance to the occupation be released promptly and unconditionally. Fair trial standards must be respected for all political detainees, including those accused of committing acts that are considered crimes according to international law.

Addameer further demands that the occupying power adhere to international law and that restrictions on the use of administrative detention be imposed. Addameer insists that the judicial review of administrative detention orders must meet the minimum international standards for due process. The authorities must provide detainees with prompt and detailed information as to the reason for their detention, and with a meaningful opportunity to defend themselves.

3. Ailing Prisoners in Israeli Occupation Jails

Health Conditions in Israeli Occupation Prisons

The health conditions in Israeli jails provided by the Israeli Prison Service (IPS) to Palestinian prisoners do not reflect the slightest respect of human rights or minimum commitment to International Humanitarian Law (IHL), but rather constitute a deliberate violation of its provisions for decent arrest conditions and proper health care.

The IPS is determined to break prisoners' immovability and resistance through a systematic policy that violates the provisions of IHL. This is demonstrated through a series of practices that includes overcrowding, poor ventilation, lack of sun exposure, limited break time, exposure to radiation, lack of cleaning supplies, lack of periodic medical examinations, psychological and physical abuse, beatings, strip searches, confinement, spray gas and deprivation of family visits. These living conditions can aggravate the physical and mental health problems of prisoners and increase the probability of catching various diseases.

This medical negligence has caused the deaths of 58 prisoners in Israeli jails, four of whom died during 2013, including Ashraf Abu Thre', Arafat Jaradat, Maysara, Abu Hamdiya, and Hassan Al-Turabi. In addition, several prisoners died after their release as a result of the diseases that they suffered from in prison, including Walid Shaath (who spent eighteen years in prison and died six months after his release), Seitan Al-Wali (who spent 23 years in prison and died after less than three years of his release), Zakariya Issa, Zuhair Lubbad, Sae'd Shamallakh, Jamil Abu Sneineh, Atef Abu Baker, Amjad Alawneh, Muslim Al-Doudi, Moussa Jum'a, Adnan Al-Balbul, Ziad Hamed, Ayed Jamjoom, and many others.

This clearly underlines the ignorance of the IPS and its medical crews to the rights of Palestinian prisoners and is a violation of the IHL and its provisions. Moreover, these acts deprive ailing prisoners of the rights granted by international conventions on human rights, especially the Standard Minimum Rules for the Treatment of Prisoners of 1957 issued by the United Nations, which stipulates (Articles 22 and 25) the need to provide at least one qualified doctor for each prison with a reasonable knowledge of psychiatry and in charge of making daily visits to ailing prisoners.[1] Article 30 of the Third Geneva Convention relative to the treatment of prisoners of war of 1949 states:

> Every camp shall have an adequate infirmary where prisoners of war may have the attention they require, as well as appropriate diet. Isolation wards shall, if necessary, be set aside for cases of contagious or mental disease. Prisoners of war suffering from serious disease, or whose condition necessitates special treatment, a surgical operation or hospital care, must be admitted to any military or civilian medical unit where such treatment can be given, even if their repatriation is contemplated in the near future. Special facilities shall be afforded for the care to be given to the disabled, in particular to the blind, and for their rehabilitation, pending their repatriation. Prisoners of war shall have the attention, preferably, of medical personnel of the Power on which they depend and, if possible, of their nationality.
>
> Prisoners of war may not be prevented from presenting themselves to the medical authorities for examination. The detaining authorities shall, upon request, issue to every prisoner who has undergone treatment, an official certificate indicating the nature of his illness or injury, and the duration and kind of treatment received. A duplicate of this certificate shall be forwarded to the Central Prisoners of War Agency. The costs of treatment, including those of any apparatus necessary for the maintenance

---

1. Standard Minimum Rules for the Treatment of Prisoners, Article 22: "At every institution there shall be available the services of at least one qualified medical officer who should have some knowledge of psychiatry. The medical services should be organized in close relationship to the general health administration of the community or nation. They shall include a psychiatric service for the diagnosis and, in proper cases, the treatment of states of mental abnormality." Article 25:"The medical officer shall have the care of the physical and mental health of the prisoners and should daily see all sick prisoners, all who complain of illness, and any prisoner to whom his attention is specially directed. The medical officer shall report to the director whenever he considers that a prisoner's physical or mental health has been or will be injuriously affected by continued imprisonment or by any condition of imprisonment."

of prisoners of war in good health, particularly dentures and other artificial appliances, and spectacles, shall be borne by the Detaining Power.

Article 13 of the same convention states:

Prisoners of war must at all times be humanely treated. Any unlawful act or omission by the Detaining Power causing death or seriously endangering the health of a prisoner of war in its custody is prohibited, and will be regarded as a serious breach of the present Convention. In particular, no prisoner of war may be subjected to physical mutilation or to medical or scientific experiments of any kind which are not justified by the medical, dental or hospital treatment of the prisoner concerned and carried out in his interest. Likewise, prisoners of war must at all times be protected, particularly against acts of violence or intimidation and against insults and public curiosity. Measures of reprisal against prisoners of war are prohibited.

Regarding the access to health care, Article 85 of the Fourth Geneva Convention, Article 29 of the Third Geneva Convention, and Articles 25 and 26 of the Standard Minimum Rules for the Treatment of Prisoners indicate the importance of providing medical services and personal hygiene.

However, the IPS policy does not take into account these legal provisions and does not provide the minimum appropriate terms and humane arrest conditions. Clinics lack specialized physicians and medical equipment. It is worth mentioning that the Ramleh prison is the only prison that has a clinic and provides medical care for patients. However, the delays in surgical procedures and the torment of ailing prisoners while being transported with no consideration to their medical status increase their suffering.

This reality explains the significant increase in the number of ailing prisoners and the acceleration in the deterioration of incurable cases. The file of ailing prisoners in Israeli jails has become the main concern of the entire prisoners' community and occupies the top priority not only to the ailing prisoners and their families but also to the political level, especially the Ministry of Prisoners' Affairs and human rights organizations working in this field.

The number of ailing prisoners has reached more than 800, including 187 prisoners with chronic diseases, 25 cancer patients, five suffering paralysis, many with amputations, 24 with mental and neurological illness, and others suffering from heart disease, kidney failure, hepatitis, osteoporosis, high blood pressure, and diabetes. Some of the critical cases are Mutassim Raddad, Mansour Mouqadeh, Yousri al-Masri, Alaa al-Hams, Khaled al-Shawish, Nahed al-Aqra', Riyad Li'mour, Muhammad Brash, Fawaz B'ara, Ibrahim Alqam, Yousef Nawaj'a, Imad Asfour, Ibrahim Al-Bitar, Murad Abu Meilq, Fuad Shobaki, Adel Arbyat, Sami I'redi, Thaer Halahalh, Nabil Natsheh, and Lina Jerboni.

The constant efforts of local, regional and international human rights organizations, and the media campaigns implemented to pressure the IPS and the Israeli government to save the lives of ailing prisoners and release critical cases, have succeeded in releasing some of them. These include Yasser Rajoub, Zakariya Issa (who died later from cancer), Mohammed al-Taj (who suffers cirrhosis of lungs and is being treated currently in Austria), and Naim al-Shawamreh (who suffers muscular dystrophy).

This means that more mass action and legal movements are needed by CSOs, the Palestinian National Authority, and Palestinian negotiators to create serious international pressure holding the Israeli government fully responsible for the lives of ailing prisoners, and to free the critical cases, and to move toward the liberation of all ailing prisoners who suffer from chronic diseases.

The daily suffering caused by the medical negligence policy practiced against Palestinian prisoners has made it necessary to focus on this urgent situation, especially as the IPS is deliberately violating all international conventions which guarantee medical care and stipulate the need of releasing chronic cases as stated in Articles 109, 110, 112, and 113 of the Third Geneva Convention and in Additional Protocol I of 1977, which applies to many prisoners in Israeli jails.

On 20 May 2010, the World Health Organization issued a decision that highlighted the ailing prisoners' situation in Israeli jails and their daily suffering. The decision demanded the International Committee of the Red Cross to form a fact-finding committee to keep a close eye on the situation of ailing prisoners and to press the Israeli government to provide the proper treatment and release critical cases. However, this decision was never implemented. It now requires exceptional efforts by Palestinian institutions to organize an international campaign pressuring the Israeli government to abide the decision and save the lives of ailing prisoners. Unless efforts are communal, the suffering of ailing prisoners will continue, and our national and human mission will be limited to diagnosis, denunciation and condemnation, while many tools and legal mechanisms are available to pressure the Israeli government to act in accordance with the provisions of international humanitarian law. In this context it is important to activate the role of medical, private, official and human rights organizations to launch a national and international campaign in order to support the ailing prisoners. This campaign must seek to:

1. Work with Palestinian political leaders for the release of the critical cases and hold the Israeli government responsible for their lives.
2. Prosecute Israeli authorities responsible for the deaths of ailing prisoners, the medical negligence policy and the lives of those who are behind bars despite the deterioration of their health condition.
3. Apply pressure on the World Health Organization to implement its decision of forming a fact-finding committee to visit Israeli prisons in an effort to improving health and living conditions of prisoners.
4. Enable a specialized medical committee to meet ailing prisoners and provide appropriate diagnosis and/or treatment to alleviate their suffering.
5. Open prison doors in front of delegations, international institutions and fact-finding committees to document the arrest and health conditions in Israeli jails.
6. Apply pressure on the IPS to provide appropriate arrest conditions aligned with relevant international standards.
7. Secure legal assistance to ailing prisoners, help them access their medical files, and provide medical reports that document their health situation.
8. Launch international campaigns to expose to the international community the suffering of the ailing prisoners and to work on the release of critical cases.

Narratives on Palestinian Prisoners and International Humanitarian Law

Medical Errors Lead to the Slow Deaths of Prisoners

The so-called medical error is another definition of the dereliction of providing ailing prisoners with the proper treatment. Prisoners' testimonies illustrate a deliberate and intentional disregard of the lives of prisoners and their health status. It shows unprofessional and irresponsible IPS medical crews providing insufficient medical care to Palestinian prisoners.

Medical errors became the basic ground of the aggravating medical negligence policy that prisoners pay for with their own health and lives. Some medical errors caused chronic diseases to prisoners, while responsible doctors have never been prosecuted for their acts.

Most of the medical crew members of IPS are new graduates who are assigned to practice in prisons without having a medical license. They practice in prison and interrogation center clinics without supervision. Facts clarify the underestimation of the ailing prisoners' situation. This unqualified crew provides treatment to prisoners without proper examination or diagnosis, sometimes by visual observation and without using medical tools. Pain killers became the magic medication provided to ailing prisoners. As a result, medical errors increase and the lives of prisoners become a target for researchers and a tool for experiments violating all conventions of human rights.

Serious legal action should be taken to monitor the professionalism of the medical staff of IPS. The World Health Organization and the Medical Unions are requested to take legal actions to question the performance of physicians practicing in IPS, given the fact that diseases are widely spread and mistaken treatments are provided among prisoners.

The absence of specialized medical staff in Israeli prisons obliged IPS to transfer ailing prisoners to civil hospitals or to the Ramleh prison clinic to take tests or do surgeries. This bureaucratic procedure is characterized by delay in taking action.

In addition, prisoners with psychological disorders or epilepsy are brutally treated; they are humiliated and kept in solitary confinement cells instead of being supervised by social and psychological counselors.

It is not possible to separate the medical errors phenomenon from the medical experimentation occurrence that was unveiled in 1997 by the Knesset member Dalia Itzik, in which the Israeli Ministry of Health gave permission to Israeli pharmaceutical companies to test several kinds of medications on prisoners. It was announced at the time that one thousand experiments were confide°ntially implemented on prisoners.

Prisoner Bassam Abu Aker stated that there is an absence of professionalism in dealing with ailing prisoners in Israeli jails. A sick prisoner has to tolerate being transported to the hospital or the Ramleh prison clinic via the so-called "Bosta."[2] The prisoner has to wait a few days in one of the sections of Ramleh prison before any test, procedure or surgery takes place. Some patients have to wait for years until a surgery is scheduled.

The IPS medical staff act as a tormentor when cooperating with the security and intelligence services, by providing medical reports that certify that prisoners are healthy enough to enable interrogators to use violence to acquire confessions. Many of IPS medical staff have blackmailed prisoners in interrogation centers, offering treatment in return for their confessions. A similar occurrence has happened with hunger strikers.

The case of Tha'er Halahlah (34 years) from Hebron is blunt evidence of the medical errors in Israeli jails. He was arrested on 9 April 2013 and was infected with hepatitis B. Tha'er testifies in an official statement:

I was transferred to the interrogation department of Askalan prison on 12 April 2013. I was forced to change my clothes to another stinky set and was escorted to the interrogation seat where I was roughly and constantly questioned. They frankly told me that they want revenge on me.

During the interrogation, I had pain in my abdomen, my teeth and my back. Despite my insistence to be seen by a doctor, interrogators refused my request and blackmailed me to confess in return for treatment.

On 16 April my pain became so severe that the interrogator called a doctor to the interrogation room. The doctor stated that I have problems

---

2. "Bosta": a designated vehicle to transfer prisoners to the military courts. It is in fact a mobile cell with a metal chair that can barely accommodate one person in a sitting position, and the windows are blacked out. The prisoner's hands and feet are cuffed so that every time the vehicle moves the cuffs leave marks on the prisoner's body. Prisoners transported in Bosta are treated without mercy and are subjected to all kinds of humiliation, verbal abuse, and mockery by the soldiers who transport them.

in the kidneys and prescribed medications that didn't improve my situation. Interrogators had to transfer me to the clinic for tests and diagnosis. At the same time I was taken to the dentist to check my swollen face. The dentist worked on repairing a filling to one of my teeth. However, I noticed through the procedure that the suction tool was stained with blood. The dentist wouldn't listen to my complaint and asked me to stay quiet.

When I was transferred to Ofer prison, the physician there tested and informed me I was infected with Hepatitis B, which can lead to liver cirrhosis and death as a result. Since then I was transferred many times to Hadassah medical center and Ramleh prison clinic for tests that recommended a special treatment, yet the only medication I got was pain killers.

Victims of Medical Negligence Policy

As per Hurryyat's documentation, 58 prisoners have lost their lives in Israeli jails due to the medical negligence policy since 1967. Many died after their release as a result to diseases they suffered from while imprisoned, including Sitan Al Wali, who spent 23 years in prison and died of cancer shortly after his release. Zakariya Issa spent ten years in jail and was released after being diagnosed with cancer that spread all over his body. Issa lost his life less than seven months after his release. Zuhair Lubbadeh was administratively detained while suffering kidney failure. His health status deteriorated during his stay in Ramleh prison clinic. He was released as soon as the IPS recognized his critical health condition to avoid being held responsibile. At that point Zuhair was in a coma. He was released and transferred to Nablus public hospital to find out that he had liver cirrhosis and pneumonia without receiving the adequate treatment in prison (while undergoing kidney dialysis procedure his hands and feet remained cuffed). Zuhair lost his battle on 31 May 2012, dying less than a week after his release.

Many other Palestinian prisoners died after their release as a result of diseases they suffered from while imprisoned, such as Said Shamlakh, Jameel abu-Sneineh, Atef abu-Baker, Amjad Alawneh, Muslem Al-Doudi, Musa Juma'a, Adnan al-Balboul, Ziad Hamed and Ayed Jamjoum.

Maysara abu-Hamdeieh: A victim of medical negligence

As narrated by fellow prisoners in Rimon, Maysara went on discontinuous hunger strikes with two other prisoners for 21 days between June and August 2011, requesting relocation from Askalan prison to another less crowded prison. In response, IPS transferred Maysara to Nafha prison, section 14. He was on four kinds of medications at that point, including for high blood pressure, high cholesterol, and stomach and diuretic medications.

Even though the Nafha prison physician strongly confirmed the necessity of Maysara's medication for his survival, the IPS eliminated his blood pressure medication, claiming that it was not available in the prison clinic pharmacy. He was given other alternative medications without checking his blood pressure, regardless of his constant requests. In other prisons, blood pressure test is a simple routine weekly test.

By the beginning of 2012, Maysara was transferred to Rimon prison, where the same alternative medication was dispensed for him. The same old medication that Maysara was taking was given to another fellow prisoner in Rimon prison; it was then that Maysara refused to take the alternative medication. The IPS provided the medication afterwards.

A short time later, a tumor was discovered in Maysara's throat. The prison's physician prescribed antibiotics only, followed by medical tests that were handed to him on 17 February 2013. Maysara requested more tests, since he was losing his vocal abilities. His nutrition was limited to soups and fluids that were vomited constantly until he lost 11 kilos. The tests were delayed and Maysara's health deteriorated.

On 10 January 2013 Maysara complained of a severe chest pain and was taken for X-ray followed by blood tests at Soroka hospital. Weekly tests were implemented until he was transferred to Eshel prison on 10 March 2013. The severe pain was preventing him from sleeping. He fell unconscious several times, got injured, and was not able to talk because of his deteriorated health conditions, as per the testimony of Rami Alami, the lawyer who visited him.

The medical committee at Soroka hospital diagnosed thyroid and throat cancer, though it never informed the patient of his situation. Rather, he was forced to endure another inhumane Bosta transport, increasing his pain.

Abu-Hamdeieh did not receive proper treatment in Eshel prison except during the last days of his life, when he was transferred to Soroka hospital as an emergency case due to a severe deterioration in his health on 30 March 2013. Maysara survived two days only and died on 2 April 2013.

His fellow prisoner Ashraf Zughayar, who accompanied Maysara through his sickness stated: "Ten days before Maysara passed away; an IPS officer called Gibzon met Maysara and was touched by the way he looked. He then told us that the law obliges the IPS to release ailing prisoners at their stages, confirming that Maysara still has time."

He added: "One day before his death, the Israeli intelligence officer Dodo came to Eshel prison and said in front of me and my colleague Saleem Juba that the prisons officer Amnon visited Maysara in the hospital where the doctors confirmed that he will be able to live for three months. He stated that his disease is at final stages and they're in the process of releasing him. Out of the ordinary a committee was established through the holiday to follow up on this matter."

The Al Ramlah passageway
This passage is taken from a prisoner's diary:

A mandatory passageway that was created for no good reason, but only to increase the pain. A long rough route that is full of hurting .... A cuffed prisoner on a metal seat, surrounded with weapons and rancorous kicks that the prison threadbare uniform won't protect from.

The prisoner passes this obligatory treatment path after the deadly wait throughout Al-Ramleh passageway. I was supposed to go to the hospital for some tests. They were supposed to heal my wounds and ease my pain. Instead, they threw me away in a bare room, bare of everything except the bitter cold of winter and the blazing heat of summer. They stopped me, rummaged through my covers, food, and medicine, and ordered me to wait in an iron cage on an iron seat in iron shackles. An hour passed, then another, until the prison officer appeared and asked: Where to? To the hospital, I said. Follow me, he said, and he led me in the opposite direction, to the passageway, for overnight. At dawn I collected my stuff and followed him, only to wait yet another hour in the cage, and be handled by another guard, and moved to another waiting room where I got to spend my day until the early hours of night. The guard called me, then slowly led me to the doctor who gave me a ice cold look, examined me, skimmed through my file and said, Come back in a month. Another night spent there, only to go back with my pains and sickness and the traces of the rough "Bosta" ride, with the memory of the crossing as a new invisible wound added to my already wounded body.

The sick prisoners in Al-Ramleh prison clinic

The sick prisoners in Al Ramleh prison clinic let out a cry through a letter addressed to the international community, urging them to intervene immediately to save the prisoners lives.

A cry of pain and for hope

We, your brothers and sick sons in the cemetery of the living write to you, out of the intensity of our pain and the severity of our suffering. With heads held high and hope that won't fade, with bodies worn out by sickness and exhaustion, we write to you longing for freedom and life, watching the anemones making their way out of an earth that longs for the footsteps of its freedom fighters. We write to you out of our pain, hoping some of us could find comfort in your support, and some of us can let out their last cry. We say, we do not fear death, otherwise we would not have faced it repeatedly in our journey to liberate our homeland and our people. We do fear, though, dying away from our loved ones, our families and our people.

Our liberation first

We write to you and we're fully aware of the efforts and struggles being made to place the prisoners cause –the sick and the old prisoners in particular—at the forefront of your national agendas, and of President Abu Mazen's attempts to highlight the cause from the rostrum of the General Assembly of the United Nations, and the persistence of our people's leadership and its various institutions and the generous efforts of the minister of prisoners affairs in highlighting our cause. Especially, emphasizing the importance of our freedom before resuming any kind of talks with the occupation that violates the standards of humanity.... This occupation exercises the worst kinds of practices, harassments and willful negligence on us. Our circumstances are worse than what our brothers in other prisons face. We are left with our pains and illnesses without real medical care. We are isolated from our other fellow prisoners in order not to create any additional reason for a clash with the IPS.

Martyrdom is our better alternative. The prisoners confirmed that the administration treats all kinds of chronic illnesses with pain killers that only threaten their lives. And they remind us of what happened to a number of prisoners that passed away as a result, including Mohammed Abu Hadwa, Jom'a Ismail, Zuheir Labade, Abdul Fattah Raddad, Murad Abu Zakour, Hayel Abu Zeid, Sitan Alwali, Abu Rizek Al'arair and Fadel Shaheen. "Martyrdom will be kinder than a situation where 16 freedom fighters live under pain, sickness and oppression. Seven of those prisoners suffer from permanent disabilities and chronic diseases, some of them end their day reciting their last will hoping they would die surrounded by their families and people."

Don't leave us alone. In their letter, the prisoners appealed to every patriot, every freedom fighter and the masses of our people that are trying to put an end to the prisoners' suffering and to deliver their message. The prisoners urge the national and Islamic parties to end the division and declare unity, in order to develop a national strategy to face the different challenges, and most importantly to support the prisoners and their liberation:

Our strength is in our unity, ending the division is necessary to liberate us. He is a criminal towards his people and cause who does not strive to bring back our unity and mobilize all our energies towards fighting our battles, succeeding for the prisoners of freedom and getting the sick prisoners out of their deathbeds, raising the Palestinian flags instead of being shrouded in them.

The sick prisoner Khalid Al-Shawish's letter to the international community

The ill prisoner Khalid Al-Shawish, who is sentenced to ten life sentences, sent a letter addressed to the international community and human rights organizations from his cell in Al Ramleh clinic, urging them to immediately intervene and pressure the Israeli government to release him and save his life and the lives of the other 16 ill prisoners in the clinic. As he says:

> Al Ramleh is not a hospital, it's a mass coffin where our wounds bleed and our lives are buried. We die silently every minute; if the walls surrounding us could speak they would shriek out of sadness and fear for our agonizing reality. Come visit our mass graves, and you'll see what you won't believe. No treatment, no doctors, nothing. Only punishment, isolation and severe pain.

Slow death. Al-Shawish pointed out that he has been held as a prisoner by the occupation for the eighth year in a row on his sickbed, on a mattress that has never been changed and that he won't ever be able to leave because he's paralyzed:

> Where are the human rights institutions? Where are the defenders of democracy? Why isn't anyone knocking on the doors of our graveyard? Until when will our isolation, our loneliness, our Nakba and our slow death in Al Ramleh clinic last?
>
> We urge anyone with some conscience left to come and visit us, and see all kinds of horror and agony. Dear inhumane world, we want you to know that Israel arrests paralyzed bodies; the wounded heals the wounded, prisoners support prisoners. We live in pain in the absence of justice, human rights and human conscience with one question haunting us: Will it ever change?
>
> Al Ramleh prison clinic is a big lie; prisoners need their health to endure the prison and its torture. How would ill and paralyzed prisoners survive? Who doesn't know the amount and quality of service needed by people with special needs? There is no special equipment or treatment here. Who would take care of us?

Al-Shawish continues:

We are tired of the slogans and statements, while death awaits us at every corner as if we were not human. We do not want medals and awards and titles. We want the simplest of our rights on this earth. We have a just cause, we did not and will not regret our sacrifices, and for that the occupation punishes us, but we will not yield. What hurts us is the injustice of human beings.

Our message is one until we get our freedom, it's a hope that we will not abandon although we were shocked by the deals that didn't save us from death. We urge you all to rise and close Al Ramleh cemetery, and transfer us to hospitals or even prisons since they are more merciful than this miserable reality of ours and our doomed fate.

The Responsibility of the International Community

The silence of the international community, including the UN organizations, toward the daily violations and suffering of prisoners is a distressful situation in the shadow with all the crimes committed by the Israeli occupation toward prisoners in Israeli jails. An immediate intervention to protect prisoners and their rights is needed at this point, especially as the international conventions of rights guaranteed the well-being of prisoners, including the Third and Fourth Geneva Conventions of 1949. It is crucial to protect prisoners and defend their national and human dignity.

In this context, prisoners responded with a comprehensive disobedience and open hunger strikes to end the injustice that threatens their lives. The previous hunger strikes were successful in drawing the attention of the international community in observing the reality of the prisoners' living conditions in Israeli jails. On the other hand, the hunger strikes deteriorated the health of prisoners and endangered their lives. The implemented hunger strikes were as follows:

- September 2011 – lasted 21 days.
- 17 April 2012 – lasted 28 days.
- Personal strikes: Khader Adnan, 66 days; Thae'r Halahla, 78 days; Hana' Shalabi, 55 days; Kifah Hattab, 31 days; Ja'far Ezzideen, 54

days, Bilal Thyab, 78 days; Hasan Safadin, 166 days; Samer al Barq, 149 days; Akram al Rikhawi, 104 days; Mahmoud Sarsak, 96 days; Omar abu Shallal, 70 days; Mohammad Taj, 67 days; Ayman Sharawnah, 157 days; and Samer Issawi, whose strike lasted nine months.

The above-mentioned facts should urge the international community to give additional attention to the suffering of prisoners and the justice of their case. Fact-finding missions are required to detect closely the reality of the living conditions of prisoners and their daily suffering. It is appropriate at this point to put pressure on the Israeli government to fulfill its commitments to the international conventions of human rights and their provisions. It is also time to highlight this humanitarian issue for people defending their freedom and fighting for their justice. Otherwise, Israel will continue practicing violations against Palestinians with no respect for international laws and absent any accountability and penalty.

We hereby direct efforts toward:

1. Expediting the formation of an international medical committee that consists of the WHO and ICRS to visit Israeli jails and observe the living and health conditions of prisoners in pursuance to the WHO resolution of 20 May 2010.
2. Requesting an immediate release of critical health cases in Israeli jails that the fact-finding mission reports, holding the Israeli government fully responsible for their well-being.
3. Cooperating with the Palestinian National Authority and international parties to appeal to the international criminal tribunals in an effort to prosecute Israeli officials responsible for Zuhair Lubbadeh's death, who was administratively detained while having kidney failure, as well as others who passed away due to the medical negligence policy.

Solitary Confinement

Solitary confinement is the most atrocious method of the medical negligence policy the IPS uses against ailing prisoners. The unhealthy living conditions that include lack of exposure to sun, humidity, spread of insects and sedentary lifestyle deteriorated the health status of many prisoners in light of the absence of adequate health care services. Solitary confinement caused Dirar al Sisi chronic diseases that he didn't have prior to isolation. Many other prisoners who suffered psychological disorders died in solitary by the acknowledgment of the IPS, such as Ra'ed abu Hammad, who died after 18 months of isolation, and Mohammad Abdeen, who died in his isolation cell on 10 June 2010 after suffering psychological problems.

Isolation is a deliberate, slow death policy that the IPS and the Israeli intelligence system commit on a daily basis against prisoners in Israeli jails. It calls for immediate intervention to condemn this policy and protect prisoners.

In 2011, three human rights organizations (Adaleh Center for Human Rights Studies, Physicians for Human Rights, and Al Mezan Center for Human Rights) published a detailed report elucidating the physical and psychological status of isolated prisoners. The report confirmed the damage on the health of the prisoners. It documented a crucial and illegal punishment against isolated humans. Isolations cells are called "alive's graves."

The tragedy of solitary confinement in Israeli jails deserves the proper attention at all levels to end the suffering of prisoners and their families. This policy should be exposed to the world, and efforts should be unified to put an end to isolation policy.

Deliberate Medical Negligence

Deliberate medical negligence policy is a crime committed against prisoners on hunger strike.

While continuing the violations of prisoners' rights, IPS pursued the medical negligence policy against prisoners on hunger strike, disregarding their lives and medical health conditions, which are deteriorating every day. Strikers were subject to assaults by IPS soldiers and officers in an effort to break their strike, as happened with Samer Isawi and Ayman Sharawnah. IPS transfers prisoners between prisons via the so-called "Busta" without justification other than to pressure strikers.

Prisoners on hunger strike are humans requesting proper living conditions or release. They are either administrative detainees or those who were re-arrested after being released through the prisoners swap in an intention to restore their previous sentence.

Occupation authorities insist on refusing the legal and just requests of prisoners on hunger strike. It is a premeditated crime committed every day against humans that needs an urgent intervention by the International Committee of the Red Cross (ICRS) and the Secretary General of the United Nations to pressure the Israeli government and hold it fully responsible for the lives of these prisoners. Israel is obliged to provide the proper health care to prisoners, especially those who went on personal or group hunger strikes against administrative detention or medical negligence policy, or who demand to be recognized as prisoners of war.

This policy was committed against prisoners Samer Isawi and Ayman Sharawnah through their open hunger strike during July and August 2012. Both prisoners were re-arrested after their release, which took place in the prisoners' swap, and were administratively detained. Their strike became the longest strike in history. Ayman exceeded seven months and Samer nine months of hunger strike, until their health situation became critical. Each lost a lot of weight and suffered pain in all parts of his body, low blood pressure and other ailments, and also the psychological pressure of refusing regular medical tests in the prison clinic as a protest to the medical negligence and mistreatment there. At an advanced stage, they discontinued taking vitamins and water.

Despite the serious and critical health situation of Samer and Ayman that led to damage of internal organs, the Israeli occupation authorities did not take action over this. Samer and Ayman were able to achieve their freedom only when the authorities agreed on nonrenewal of their administrative detention and not restoring their previous sentence.

In regards to the group strike that took place on 17 April 2012, requesting the elimination of solitary confinement and allowing family visits to Gaza prisoners, Israel's position at the international level was not at its best during this time. The Israeli government drafted a proposed bill that would allow the force-feeding of Palestinian political prisoners on hunger strike. The proposed bill by the Justice Ministry as well as security and intelligence agencies, is clearly designed to subdue the prisoners. The IPS and its special units continued to take extreme punitive measures against the hunger strikers in an attempt to break their strike regardless of the necessity of protecting the rights of hunger strikers in accordance with International Humanitarian Law and International Human Rights Law.

Force-feeding of hunger strikers jeopardizes the survival of those prisoners as well as breaches their dignity. The awful previous experiences caused the deaths of three prisoners: Abdul Qader Abul Fahm, Ali Jafari, and Rasem Halawah. Force-feeding entails forcing a rubber tube into the prisoner's mouth or nostril, pressing it all the way down until it reaches the esophagus. This causes a lot of suffering to hunger strikers and sometimes leads to death.

The Prisoner Priority

Freeing ailing prisoners from Israeli occupation jails is the first national priority for the Palestinian people and the prisoners' movement.

Losing the lives of four prisoners in less than a year as a result of the medical negligence policy proved an alarming threat and concern among the prisoners' movement, their families and the whole Palestinian society at all levels. Ashraf Abu Thrai, Arafat Jaradat, Maysara Abu Hamdeieh and Hasan Turabi were the victims of the Israeli Prison Service and its medical team, who refused to provide them with the proper treatment or release them despite their knowledge of the critical health these prisoners were facing. Many other prisoners have cancer, heart disease, disability and other chronic diseases; however, they hardly get the minimum treatment.

In an effort to disrupt the medical negligence policy, the prisoners' movement performed a series of actions entitled: "Save the lives of ailing prisoners before it is too late." Actions included strong letters sent to IPS and the Israeli government holding them fully responsible for the lives of ailing prisoners.

Similarly, ailing prisoners in Ramleh clinic expressed their willingness to start an open food and medication strike demanding their release. Their suffering and their unattainable hopes of freedom (after previous swap deals ignored their case) forced them to take action, so they would not face the destiny of those who had already lost their lives.

It is important to highlight that the freedom of ailing prisoners is not the responsibility of the prisoners' movement nor the ailing prisoners themselves. It also is the responsibility of the Palestinian people in general, those on the political level and the Palestinian negotiator. Previous achievements such as the prisoners swap deals and the hunger strike of 2012 that released isolated prisoners from solitary confinements placed the issue of ailing prisoners at the top of national priorities. Therefore, it is important at this point that the Palestinian negotiator give special attention to this issue within any peace negotiation process and raise it in the international arena without delay. This should be parallel to other national and international media campaigns that expose Israeli violations to the international communities, in order to hold the Israeli government fully responsible for the lives of ailing prisoners. International fact-finding missions are indispensable to acquaint the public with the reality of the crimes committed against prisoners behind bars. Criminals should be subject to prosecution by the international courts.

Releasing Ailing Prisoners Is a Legitimate Right

In light of the deteriorating health conditions of ailing prisoners and the deaths of four of them in less than one year, the prisoners issue has recently become one of the most important. Eight hundred Palestinian and Arab prisoners in Israeli jails suffer various diseases; 200 of these suffer severe deterioration in their health conditions caused by lack of proper health care. Most common of all is cancer, heart disease, kidney failure, diabetes and spine problems.

Ailing prisoners are suffering inhumane conditions that directly affect their lives because of deliberate negligence of their basic humanitarian right to get proper heath care similar to that delivered to Israeli citizens.

Despite the efforts that were carried out by national and international human rights organizations, including WHO and ICRC, demanding the proper health care for ailing prisoners, the Israeli authorities and the IPS have not improved the health status of prisoners; rather they increased their suffering and put their lives in real danger.

The Third and Fourth Geneva conventions of 1949 and the UN Standard Minimum Rules for the Treatment of Prisoners (1957) guaranteed the proper health care and suitable living conditions; in particular, articles 31 and 92 of the Third Geneva Convention assure a monthly medical exam of prisoners to monitor their health status, including x-rays at least once a year. However, the Israeli authorities evade their commitments toward these conventions by limiting health care services to ailing prisoners, causing slow death of targeted prisoners and ignoring their right to live and receive the proper health care services.

In regards to the medical requirements and access to doctors, article 82 of the Fourth Geneva Convention and article 29 of the Third Geneva Convention assured the importance of providing health facilities and maintained sanitation. Article 30 of the Third Geneva Convention states: "Prisoners of war may not be prevented from presenting themselves to the medical authorities for examination. The detaining authorities shall, upon request, issue to every prisoner who has undergone treatment, an official certificate indicating the nature of his illness or injury, and the duration and kind of treatment received." Articles 109 and 110 of the Third Geneva Convention and the additional protocol 1 state that prisoners with critical health situation should be returned to their countries of origin.

The Israeli violations of prisoner rights in general and ailing prisoner rights in particular are a deliberate violation against human rights and IHL. Thus, we urge countries that signed the Geneva Conventions to collaborate and take measures that oblige Israel to commit to providing the proper treatment to ailing prisoners and release critical cases to avoid their death as previously explained.

The Most Critical Cases in Israeli Jails
Riyad Li'mour
Name: Riyad Dakhlallah Ahmad Li'mour
City: Taqqou' - Bethlehem
Date of Birth: June 18, 1971
Date of Arrest: May 7, 2002
Sentence: Life
Marital Status: Married, with five children

As one of the most wanted by the Israeli occupation military forces, Riyad Li'mour was arrested in 2002 after three years of pursuit. He was sentenced to 99 years of prison.

Riyad is held in Ramleh prison permanently for his critical health situation. He was suffering a heart muscle weakness when arrested and digestion problems caused by a previous gunshot injury in the abdomen. The severe injury caused the eradication of part of the intestines, part of his liver as well as part of the pyloric sphincter. The deliberate medical negligence in the Israeli jails increased his suffering. Riyad did not receive medical tests or follow-up for a long time, which deteriorated his health situation to a critical point. He is now living on a pacemaker device that has needed replacement for several years. He passes out regularly and remains pale and tired.

Li'mour's health situation is considered the most critical in Ramleh prison based on the clinic's physicians' assessment. The patient is unable to bathe without the support of others, fearing his passing out and falling. He also suffers nausea, headache and a high proportion of body fluids not allowing him to sleep in a straight position. Riyad is unable to sleep without analgesic drugs. On 19 June 2013, Riyad entered an open hunger strike in protest against the medical negligence policy against him and other ailing prisoners. As a result, his health situation deteriorated critically. He was transferred to Assaf Harofeh Medical Center where his pacemaker was replaced. However, Riyad's state of health was instable, as he was suffering arteries blockage. An open heart surgery was implemented in Tel Hashomer Hospital on 17 October 2012, and he was transferred to Ramleh prison clinic few days after his surgery. The late intervention of the IPS towards treating Riyad led to deteriorating his health to a critical situation. His life is in danger and he needs a permanent and intensive health care.

Khaled Shaweesh

Name: Khaled Jamal Mousa Al Shaweesh
City: O'uqaba - Toubas
Date of Birth: January 14, 1971
Date of Arrest: May 28, 2007
Sentence: Life
Marital Status: Married, with four children

Khaled was well known to the Israeli occupation forces as a military operations activist during the second Intifada. His struggle against occupation extended to the Ramallah area, where he was chased for several years.

In 2002 the Israeli occupation forces invaded Ramallah, and Khaled was shot in the abdomen during a fire exchange with the Israelis. The injury caused severe damage of his intestines, fractured four spinal vertebrae and caused obstruction in his hand and permanent paralysis. Khaled was besieged with President Arafat in the Ramallah Headquarters and got arrested in 2007 while he was hospitalized and was sentenced to life in prison. He exists at present in the Ramleh prison clinic.

As a result of the mentioned injury, splinters settled in different parts of his body including the spine and caused him restless sleeping or sitting positions. Skin blisters are all over his body. The only treatment Khaled gets is a monthly muscle relaxing shot that reduces his pain. The IPS closed Khaled's medical file claiming that he is not responding the treatment, yet continued exposing him to all kinds of abuse that included strip searching. He submitted a claim against the IPS but with no positive results.

All requests submitted by Khaled and his family to be treated in external clinics other than the prison clinic or to be examined by a Palestinian physician were refused; the only service Khaled received was an x-ray. Khaled's health is deteriorating; he suffers shortness of breath, headaches, and lack of sleep.

Mansour Mouqadeh

Name: Mansour Mohammad Abdul Aziz Nimr Mouqadeh
City: Salfeet – Al Zawyeh
Date of Birth: February 17, 1968
Date of Arrest: July 1, 2002
Sentence: 35 Years
Marital Status: Married, with four children

Mansour was arrested in an exchange of fire in Sannirya village 11 years ago. He was shot with six bullets in the chest and abdomen. Not only had the soldiers left him bleeding, but they also beat him on the wounds. Mansour went into a coma for three months after being transferred to Ramleh prison clinic. Five surgeries followed, removing his bladder, his stomach and his intestines and installing a synthetic stomach and intestines. He lives now on an ostomy pouching system, since he is not able to control his excretory or urinary systems, for he suffers sensory loss in the lower part of the body that is also paralyzed.

In addition to this, Mansour suffers shortness of breath and numbness in different parts of the body. He is in urgent need of implanting an artificial urinary bladder and neurosurgery to help him control his urinating and defecating. Recently; a three-centimeter lump appeared in the lower right side of his neck.

When taken to the hospital half dead, the nurse stared at him and yelled: "Why didn't you die?" Mansour replied: "Death can wait until I put my air shoes on and get up. Nothing prevents the place from waiting until the sky carries me to my destiny."[3]

Mutasem Raddad

Name: Mutasem Taleb Daoud Raddad
City: Tulkarm - Saida
Date of Birth: November 11, 1982
Date of Arrest: January 12, 2006
Sentence: 20 Years
Marital Status: Single

Mutasem was the target of an assassination attempt in Jenin prior to his arrest, which left his body riddled with splinters. As a result, he suffered pain in the chest, lack of breath and coughing up blood. The suffering continued when he started getting a high temperature and loss of appetite until he got emaciated. It took the Israeli Prison Services six months to allow a specialist in Ramleh prison clinic to see him and examine him. Then the results of the tests took three months to be sent back to the Ramleh prison.

Mutasem is suffering recently from blood in his stool and a noticeable weight loss. The prison doctor advised a boiled-food-based diet, which the IPS did not commit to. He was transferred to different hospitals for examination and was diagnosed with bowel cancer. A cortisone medication was prescribed for him as a pain relief, but it is not effective anymore because of the consistent use.

---

3. Issa Qaraqeh Article – the place can wait until you stand up.

In addition to all the suffering, Mutasem took heart injections that proved of no benefit. His blood pressure became irregular, and his heartbeat rose to 120 beats a minute. The malfunction of the blood sugar that he also suffered caused him another weight loss. He is anemic and suffers consistent high body temperature.

Mutasem is now taking a three-hour session of chemotherapy every six weeks. Despite his critical health situation, he is transported to his session through the "Bosta" (a three-hour journey of suffering), which led him to start an open hunger strike and refrain from his medication, requesting proper transport to the chemotherapy session through a regular car.

Recently, his medication dose was increased to include antibiotics, heart and nerve medications, in addition to increasing his chemotherapy dose. Mutasem is also anemic and his health is deteriorating every day.

Prisoner Mutasem and his prison mates are approaching the humanitarian organizations and the international community to intercedeto provide him with help in his treatment and/or release him to save his life.

Nahed Aqra'
Name: Nahed Faraj Jaddou' Aqra'
City: Gaza
Date of Birth: January 8, 1968
Date of Arrest: July 11, 2007
Sentence: 99 Years
Marital Status: Married, with four children

Nahed spent 10 years of a life sentence in Israeli jails before being released through the Oslo agreement in 1993. He served in the security services in Gaza but was kidnapped during the coup d'état and shot in the legs.

He was transferred afterward to Egypt for treatment, then to Jordan, where his right leg was amputated. The Israeli occupation forces arrested him in 2007 on his way back to Gaza through the West Bank. He was accused of being responsible for exploding an Israeli Merkava in Gaza – Al Mintar area. He went through interrogation and was sentenced to life imprisonment.

For six consecutive years, Nahed has been detained in Ramleh prison clinic in his electric wheel chair. The medical negligence policy of the Israeli

Prison Services has exacerbated his health situation, especially as he had splinters in his left leg that caused him strapping pain; however all the pain killers and sleeping pills that he had were of no effect. Nahed ended up with decomposition of flesh around his wounds, and his left leg was amputated in April 2013. However, he is still suffering infections in his left leg and it was advised that further amputation take place.

Nahed has been deprived of visits from his family in Gaza since he was arrested. His father died few months ago, while his old mother who lives in the West Bank is the only one who can visit him. He pursued a hunger strike on 25 July 2013 in response to the tragic situation of the ailing prisoners and to highlight the ailing prisoners' right to live before it is too late.

Alaa' Al Hams
Name: Alaa' Ibrahim Ali al Hams
City: Gaza
Date of Arrest: January 24, 2009
Sentence: 29 Years
Marital Status: Single

Alaa' al Hams is a 40-year-old prisoner who suffers tuberculosis, a disease that causes constant coughing and emaciation of the body. He was treated at Khadira hospital with a medication that had severe side effects on him. Alaa' developed a tumor in the right thyroid lobe, stomach hernia and micturition reflex.

Al Hams developed severe intestinal infection that causes him to vomit blood, and sometimes he wakes up with blood filling his mouth. This has caused occasional comatose condition and limited his talking abilities. He has also lost 80 percent of the vision in his left eye.

In one of his testimonies, on 12 December 2013, Alaa' stated that he had a strong pain in stomach and requested a visit to the prison's clinic. The answer Alaa' received was that the doctor was busy. Twenty minutes later the doctor escorted Alaa' to the examination room with the prison representative Mohammad Zawahreh. The doctor and the nurse denigrated his situation, which got him nervous and caused his hands and feet to spasm. His blood pressure and he had shortness of breath. The doctor had to give him a shot and medication to calm him down.

During this time; Alaa' asked for water that was handed out to him in a urine test cup. Alaa' refused to drink and his fellow prisoner Zawahreh pointed to this behavior as a humiliating act. As a result he was taken back to the prison cell and Alaa' was kicked out of the clinic while in seizure without respect. Alaa' testified that the doctor pulled him up by his shirt and cruelly threw him on the ground.

Yusri Al Masri

Name: Yusri Ateyya Mohammad Al Masri
City: Deir Al Balah - Gaza
Date of Birth: March 23, 1983
Date of Arrest: June 9, 2003
Sentence: 20 years
Marital Status: Single

Yusri was transferred from Nafha prison to Ramleh prison clinic after being medically neglected and not receiving proper treatment for his thyroid cancer. The patient was healthy upon his arrest, but started having headaches, fever, and abdominal pain. Several tests were taken to diagnose his problem at Nafha prison; however the prison doctor did not inform Yusri that he has a thyroid problem. The only treatment he received was pain killers.

After the severe deterioration in his health situation, Yusri was transferred to Soroka hospital where a cancerous tumor was found in his thyroid gland and a hypertrophy lymphoid to 17 millimeters that also spread to different parts of his body and caused him a 15 kilo weight loss. The doctors had no choice except of setting a surgery to remove the tumor and prevent its expansion.

He was handcuffed during the operation, and transferred to Ramleh prison clinic three days after surgery, despite the doctors' orders that he be kept longer in the hospital. The transfer took place in the "Bosta" instead of an ambulance, without regard to his critical health situation.

Yusri is frequently exposed to medical negligence in Ramleh prison clinic; he personally changes the surgical incision dressing, and he is not taking any chemotherapy, calcium or thyroid medication that was prescribed in Soroka hospital. Yusri is calling for all human rights organizations to support him and prevent him from facing the same destiny of Hasan Turabi, for he would rather die among his family members.

Emad Asfour

Name: Emad Rajeh Abdul Latif Asfour
City: Ya'bad - Jenin
Date of Birth: February 27, 1974
Date of Arrest: January 24, 2001
Sentence: 15 years
Marital Status: married, with two children

Born in Ya'bad, Emad joined the resistance forces at early age. He was arrested in 1991 for the first time and was sentenced to six months in prison. After his release he completed his high school and nursing diploma. Emad was arrested again and was roughly interrogated so that his health deteriorated and he was transferred to Ramleh prison clinic where he spent his two-year sentence.

During the second Intifada, Emad was listed on the wanted list of Israeli occupation authorities. He survived several murder attempts until he was arrested for the third time on 24 January 2001.

Emad was kept in Mascobeia interrogation center for 90 days, upon which his health deteriorated without receiving the proper treatment. He was sentence to 15 years in prison.

The cruel interrogation, the long arrest with no health care and the deliberate medical negligence deteriorated his health to a critical situation. Emad has high blood pressure and pulse, strong headaches that prevent him from eating and sleeping, and high cholesterol causing blockage in the heart valves. A catheterization procedure was implemented on him at the Soroka hospital after having a heart attack on 4 September 2013, which aggravated his situation.

4. Families and Family Visits

Over 5,000 Palestinian political prisoners are currently being held in Israeli prisons and are often denied their basic human rights. One of the many rights they have been denied is their right to communicate with their families and receive regular visits. Imprisonment causes a huge amount of suffering and hardship, not only for those denied of their liberty, but for their relatives on the outside. Whole families and generations have grown up with no mother or father or brother or sister. The Israeli policy of mass detention and imprisonment has been devastating for Palestinian society, with families of prisoners being the silent victims.

Family visits are routinely, and often arbitrarily, restricted or cancelled by the Israeli authorities. Moreover, many Arab-Israeli, West Bank prisoners and Gaza prisoners are denied their visitation rights completely. This is in complete contradiction with Israel's responsibility, as the Occupying Power, under international law. The right to family visits is an entrenched right in international law, expressly provided for in the Fourth Geneva Convention, the Standard Minimum Rules for the Treatment of Prisoners, the Body of Principles for the Protection of All Persons under Any Form of Detention or Imprisonment, the European Prison Rules, and, in relation to child detainees, the Convention on the Rights of the Child.

Israel detains Palestinians from the occupied Palestinian territory in detention centers outside 1967 occupied territory. This practice is illegal under international law and poses significant challenges to Palestinian prisoners' ability to receive family visits as they must acquire permits to enter Israel in order to visit their relatives in prison. In many cases these permits are extremely difficult to obtain, while in many others cases they are impossible to obtain. Israel always gives the same reason for not issuing permits — "security" — but never defines what this means.

When family visits are able to take place, severe restrictions are placed on them by the Israeli Prison Service. Only first-degree relatives may visit, but any male family member aged between 16 and 35 is typically prevented from visiting. Once at the prison, family members can only expect to communicate with their loved ones from behind glass separation walls or by telephone.

For Palestinian prisoners from Gaza, the situation is particularly dire: prior to 2007, they were permitted family visits, but following the 2006 Palestinian election results and the capture of Israeli soldier Gilad Shalit, Israel denied residents of Gaza held in Israeli prisons family visits due to "unspecified security reasons," a measure that can be understood as collective punishment of the Gaza population. On 9 December 2009, the Israeli High Court of Justice rejected an appeal contesting the policy's legality.

During Palestinian prisoners' mass hunger strike in April 2012, one main demand of the prisoners was to reinstate family visits to Gaza prisoners. Though Israel agreed to resume the visits upon the conclusion of the hunger strike, as of June 2014, these visits have taken place every two months, as opposed to every two weeks for prisoners from the West Bank, Jerusalem and 1948 territories.

The Process of Family Visits

Until the outbreak of the Al-Aqsa Intifada in September 2000, family visits to Palestinian detainees held in Israeli prisons were regular and took place largely without interruptions. However, following the Israeli re-invasion of the West Bank and as a result of imposed movement restrictions, all Palestinian families from the occupied territory who wish to visit a family member detained in Israel – with the exception of Jerusalem ID holders – must receive an entry permit into Israel.

The application process is lengthy and can take between one and three months, while the permit itself is valid for only one year. The application is submitted via the International Committee of the Red Cross (ICRC) and then transferred to the Israeli authorities. Visits are restricted to first degree relatives – children, spouses, parents, siblings and grandparents only, thus isolating the detainee from his or her social and professional environment. As mentioned, men between the ages of 16 and 35 are typically prevented from visiting prison and receive special permits only once a year if they are the brother of the detainee and bi-annually if they are the son of the detainee. In practice, however, hundreds of families fail to receive permits at all, based on "security grounds." The reason for the rejection of a permit application is never given apart from the standard phrase: "forbidden entry into Israel for security reasons."

When family visits are allowed, they take place once every two weeks for 45 minutes. In the visiting room, a glass window separates the visitor and the prisoner. Communication takes place through a telephone or through holes in the glass. For every prisoner, only three adults and two minors are allowed to visit at the same time.

Case Study: The Nasser Family

"We leave with eyes full of tears and a heart full of hope, a hope for freedom."

Thabet Nassar (35), from Nablus, is a husband and a father of three children and has been imprisoned seven times over the last 15 years. His first imprisonment was in August 1998, and the latest in November 2013. When not imprisoned, Thabet works as a nurse in Rafedia's public hospital and pursues a degree in public health administration at Al-Quds Open, University. Yet, due to the repeated arrests and imprisonment Thabet has been unable to complete his undergraduate studies. Although Thabet has been married for the past seven years, he has actually lived no more than a couple of years with his wife and children.

The repeated arrests and detention of Thabet have not only caused great hardship on his part, but also had a great impact on his family. Thabet's three children, Yamen (6), Amal (4) and Mais (8 months), have grown up with the absence of their father which has caused them great suffering. Yamen and Amal were both born while their father was in prison, while Mais was born on the day of her father's latest arrest. The children grew up not knowing their father very well, and are constantly asking their mothers questions about their father that she falls short on answering like, "Why is our father imprisoned?" and "Why can't he come home with us?"

Nassar's family encounters tremendous difficulties while trying to visit him in prison. The first time Nassar's wife, Rana, visited him was after his arrest in 2007, the same year they got married. Rana first applied for a permit and obtained it through the ICRC. However, after two visits, the permit was confiscated from her by Israeli Occupying Forces at Taybeh checkpoint. Following that, Rana tried again to obtain a permit, but was denied due to "security reasons." However, Nassar's mother and children are allowed to visit him.

Following the latest arrest of Nassar in 2013, Rana was able to obtain a permit to visit. Rana describes the visits as "a painful journey filled with suffering and humiliation." The visit takes a full day, as they leave their homes to take the bus at 6:00 a.m., wait for hours at checkpoints and are exposed to "humiliating body searches and security inspections." Upon their arrival to the prison, they are searched again, and then taken to the visitation room where they are only allowed 45 minutes with Nassar.

According to Rana, communication with her husband during the visit is very difficult as they are separated by a glass barrier, and are only allowed to speak through broken phones which make it very difficult to hear each other. Communication is even more difficult as there are ten families in each visitation room, leaving no room for any privacy with their imprisoned relatives. Furthermore, the children are only allowed to have physical contact with their father once a year. Leaving the visitation room is often a very emotional moment for the whole family. Rana describes it by saying, "We leave with eyes full of tears and a heart full of hope, a hope for freedom." They are then forced to wait until all of the visits are over, since all of the families have to leave together, usually reaching their homes at night.

Palestinian Women's Detention and the Family

The conditions of arrest and detention of Palestinian women political prisoners affect women individually and also serve as a form of collective punishment against their entire family. Consider, for instance, the case-study of Qahira Saeed As-Saadi. After arresting two other members of the As-Saadi family the previous day, the Israeli Occupying Forces returned on 8 May 2002 to arrest Qahira. After having experienced the trauma of witnessing their two uncles detained, Qahira's four children were again forced to watch as their mother was assaulted and detained by Israeli troops. All too often, such incidents of violence during arrest have an enormous psychological impact on the children who witness them.

After being brought to the Al Moskobiyyeh interrogation centre in Jerusalem, Qahira was subjected to further physical and psychological torture, including bodily and verbal abuse. Of particular concern, Qahira was told that her 10- and 16-year-old daughters had also been arrested and would be raped unless Qahira complied with the prison authorities' demands. Qahira's children were prevented from visiting their mother for the first two years of her imprisonment. Her oldest daughter was repeatedly denied a permit to visit on "security grounds." The children were allowed to spend only half an hour with their mother even though the entire trip to the prison and back takes them around ten hours because of extreme delays caused by continual baggage and body searches. During the visit, the children were separated from their mother by a big glass divider and could not touch her; instead, they were forced to speak to their mother through telephones.

In addition to the impact of inadequate family contact on the children of women prisoners, such conditions have compounding effects on the psychological and physical well-being of women in prison. Research has shown that the prohibition of family visits for women in prison often leads to conditions of anxiety and depression and exacerbates feelings of isolation. While visits to Palestinian prisoners are currently permitted twice a month in theory, prisoners and family members are subjected to many restrictions stemming from Israel's practice of detaining Palestinian prisoners outside 1967 occupied territory, in violation of Article 76 of the Fourth Geneva Convention (1949), which explicitly prohibits "individual or mass forcible transfers, as well as deportations of protected persons from occupied territory to the territory of the Occupying Power."

The maintenance of ties between family members is overly dependent on the Israeli permit system, which imposes huge restrictions on the Palestinian population – especially males – aged between 16 and 45, whose right to visit are denied on a regular basis. As demonstrated in the case of Qahira and her family, the restrictions on visitation rights not only violate the United Nations Standards Minimum Rules for the Treatment of Prisoners but have lasting and compounding effects on the entire family.

Case Study: The Sayyad Family

"Don't cry because I love you and I am always here for you."

Upon her arrest on 22 November 2012, Entesar Sayyad (38) was separated from her four children, causing great hardship to her and her children. Following her arrest, Entesar was held in and transferred between several prisons. She was first held in Al-Moskobiyya, a notorious detention center in Jerusalem, for thirteen days before being transferred to Neve Titzra women's prison in Ramleh where she remained for one month. On 20 January 2013 she was finally transferred to HaSharon prison. Before being sentenced her family was only able to see her from a distance at the court hearings; and they were only able to visit her three months after her initial arrest.

International Law on Family Visits

Israel constantly breaches international law by continuously denying prisoners from receiving family visits. Prisoners' right of receiving family visits and having proper communication with their families is deeply rooted in international law. It was clearly defined in Article 116 of the Fourth Geneva Convention (1949) that internees are entitled to the right of receiving family visits on a frequent basis and at 'regular intervals.' The Standard Minimum Rules for the Treatment of Prisoners (1977) also states in Articles 37 and 92 that prisoners have the right to communicate with their families and 'reputable friends' through correspondence and by receiving visits. The right of prisoners to receive family visits is further emphasized in the Body of Principles for the Protection of All Persons under Any Form of Detention or Imprisonment (1988) which states that prisoners and detainees should be given the right to be visited by their families under 'reasonable conditions and restrictions.' International law also stresses the rights of minors to receive family visits in the UN Rules for the Protection of Juveniles Deprived of their Liberty (1990). Articles 59 and 60 clearly define minors rights in communicating with the 'wider community,' and receiving family visits on a regular and a frequent basis, ideally once a week or at least once a month.

Like other families Entesar's family faces great hardships during visits to the prison. Her children are only allowed to visit her twice a month, for 45 minutes. According to her youngest son, Ibrahim, "going to visit is very exhausting and tiring because of the long distances [they have to travel]." Her daughter, Dania, insists on visiting her mother despite the motion sickness she has to endure on the way to the prison. Upon their arrival at the prison, her children are forced to wait for long hours until they are finally allowed to see their mother, due to the fact that female prisoners' visits take place only after the minors and male prisoners' visits are over. The children are searched twice before they are allowed into the visitation room. Yet, the children feel that the hardest part about the visits is that they are not allowed to have any physical contact with their mother, and instead are forced to communicate through glass barriers. Entesar's daughter, Malak, adds, "I cannot hug or even touch my mother due to the glass barrier between us."

Entesar herself finds it very difficult to see her children through the glass barrier only, as she really wishes she can hold her children in her arms. She tries to remain strong in front of them but cries after each visit. She plans ahead what she wants to tell them, yet forgets all the words when she sees them. Her son Ibrahim (12) recalls that during their first visit to their mother she looked pale and started crying when she saw them. Attempting to make his mother feel better, Ibrahim told her, "Don't cry because I love you and I am always here for you." Entesar and her children also find it difficult to exchange letters as they don't get delivered for a long time or don't get delivered at all.

Entesar's imprisonment has had a severe impact on the children, emotionally, and particularly with their education. The children are constantly missing their mother's presence around them; her daughter Malak found her graduation very painful without her mother being there, while all of her classmates' mothers were in attendance. Not only are they emotionally impacted, but their schoolwork has been affected by their mother's imprisonment and the family visits. Following his mothers' arrest and imprisonment, Ibrahim's academic performance was affected, leading his father to hire a private tutor to help him. And since Monday is the only day they are allowed to visit their mother, they have to skip a school day every two weeks.

Yet, the children continue to be hopeful, stating that they are very proud of their mother, and are waiting impatiently for her release.

On 9 June 2014 Entesar was released from prison and reunited with her family.

Reintegration and Life after Prison

Social reintegration of prisoners includes rehabilitation during and after imprisonment by ensuring access to Palestinian-administered social services, as well as immediate and long-term post-release support. The issue of reintegration of Palestinian prisoners is unique in the sense that it is affected by two authorities that are in conflict with one another in the midst of an unequal distribution of power, where one authority is occupied by the other. Although the UN Minimum Standard Rules for the Treatment of Prisoners recommend that "necessary steps be taken to ensure for the prisoner a gradual return to life in society" through a pre-release programme, Israel denies such services to Palestinian prisoners.

Moreover, a number of the key issues that affect a prisoner's life after release and inadvertently determine the success of his/her rehabilitation process are controlled by Israeli authorities, including the quality of prison conditions and safety in prison, which can have lasting effects on a prisoner's mental and physical health, access to education resources, adequate contact with the outside world, specialist medical care and nutritional support. These issues, among others, are explicitly a matter of Israeli responsibility, and Israeli authorities largely fail to provide for these rights.

It is important to note, however, that these rights and services must be administered only by Palestinians; as such, the Israeli authorities and the IPS must grant full, unhindered access to Palestinian programs and service providers in this regard. Israel's failure to provide full access to these rights and services undermines the process of creating a long-term post-release strategy for Palestinian women prisoners.

Interviews conducted with former Palestinian women prisoners by both Addameer and the Palestinian Counseling Center (PCC) revealed that these women are in great need of psychological support especially in the first weeks and months following their release. The lack of services and support mechanisms during their prison experience and upon their release, combined with the overwhelming initial media interest, only exacerbates ex-prisoners' feelings of disappointment and isolation, which can often lead to an increase in mental health concerns.

The transition from life in prison to life outside is therefore even more problematic. At a workshop held by the PCC on 16 August 2008 in Ramallah to assess former women prisoners' needs, a call for psycho-social support was reiterated by many participants. Former Palestinian women prisoners affirmed at the workshop that a holistic approach to pre- and post-release programs needs to be developed in order to include their families in support schemes.

Some of the initiatives provided by the Ex-Detainees Rehabilitation Programme, until recently operated by the Palestinian Ministry of Detainees and Ex-Detainees, include educational assistance, vocational training, wage subsidies, self-employment loans, project loans and health insurance. However, to date there has been no long-term, gender-specific reintegration and rehabilitation programmes established by the Ministry. While a special unit has been established to deal with youth and child detainees, no such facility for women has yet been created. In addition, although the legal section of the Child and Youth Unit created by the Ministry provides legal counseling to women prisoners along with child detainees, this support and interest stops once the woman is released.

Case Study: The Sa'adat Family

Popular Front for the Liberation of Palestine (PFLP) Secretary General Ahmad Sa'adat (61) was arrested by Israel on 14 March 2006 when he was taken from the Palestinian Authority's Jericho prison in a raid by Israeli Occupying Forces. Two years later, he was sentenced to 30 years. Ahmed is married to Abla (58) and has four children: Ghassan (32), Ibaa (29), Sumoud (28) and Yaser (23).

Two members of the family, Alba and Ghassan, are Jerusalem ID holders, while the rest of the family are West Bank ID holders. The practical implications of this means they have to apply for a permit to enter 1948 Territories to visit their father in prison. However, holding a Jerusalem ID does not automatically entitle a person to visit as it is left to the discretion of the Israeli authorities. This has been the experience of Ahmed's wife Alba who, since 2008, has been regularly denied visits to her husband. A recent example of this occurred in March 2014, when she arrived at the prison only to be told by prison officials that she is banned from visiting. As of June 2014 this ban remains in place.

West Bank ID holders Ibaa and Yaser have visited their father only once since the beginning of his imprisonment in 2006, as all other attempts to visit their father have been denied on "security" grounds, although the Israeli authorities never give any further explanation. Another daughter Sumoud has never visited her father in prison, again based on undefined "security" grounds.

In March 2008, Sa'adat received an order to be placed in isolation for six months, which was subsequently renewed every six months for over three years. During this time no family member was allowed to visit.

When visits are allowed, they are extremely difficult due to the Israeli procedures involved. For example, family members with West Bank ID holders are picked up in ICRC buses at 6.00 a.m. in Ramallah. Before entering 1948 Territories they must pass through Beit Seira' checkpoint, where they wait for about two hours. During this time family members must undergo electronic and physical searches. Once they arrive at the prison they must pass through more security checks, electronic and physical checks by prison guards. It is common for families to wait for up to five hours before they can actually enter the prison. Once they enter they must wait for usually 45 minutes in the waiting room, which have no restrooms or drinking water.

When the visit actually begins, the family must communicate through a glass divider, using a telephone. The phones are usually damaged and therefore the quality of the sound in not good. It is also not unusual for the guards to delay bringing Ahmed to the visiting room which limits the time the family has to see him. The absence of Amhed has caused great hardship for the family, particularly for his wife Abla as she must play the role of both mother and father. For the family occasions of celebration, like birthdays and weddings, are particularly difficult and there is always an increased sense of sadness and loss.

Conclusion

Israel's policy of mass detention and imprisonment has had a devastating and immeasurable impact on Palestinian society. Given that Israel has detained or imprisoned approximately 750,000 Palestinian since 1967, one can only begin to imagine the effects that this had had on the families of those imprisoned. It is very difficult to find any household in Palestine that has not been affected by detention and imprisonment; this is one of the reasons why the prisoners are so close to people's hearts in Palestine.

According to international law all those detained are entitled to family visits. However, Israel continues to systematically deny these visits as a punitive measure, meaning that some family members have not seen their imprisoned relatives in years. In breach of international law Israel holds the vast majority of Palestinian political prisoners inside Israel. The practical consequence of this is that most Palestinians from the OPT must apply for an entry permit to visit their relatives in prison. These permits are regularly denied on "security grounds" although Israel never defines what this means.

One only has to look at the mass hunger strikes of mid-2014 involving over 125 administrative detainees to see how Israel uses family visits as a punitive measure. Immediately following the launch of the strike all family visits for the hunger strikers were banned for four months, while the leaders of the hunger strike were banned for six months. The banning of family visits was one of many punitive measures taken by the Israeli authorities against the hunger strikers.

However, the untold story remains that of the families who have had to endure so many years without their relatives. Not only have they witnessed their mothers, fathers, brothers and sisters being violently arrested by a brutal occupying power but they have been also denied the ability to visit them once imprisoned. All the memories that most people take for granted are filled with sadness and sorrow for the families of the prisoners – birthdays, weddings, anniversaries – all are never really what they should be. For the families of the prisoners these memories will always be a time of mixed emotions until the day the prisoners are released and reunited once again.

5. Palestinian Children Detained in the Israeli Military Court System

Palestinian child prisoners continue to be systematically ill-treated during their arrest, transfer and interrogation. This treatment consists of physical violence and verbal abuse, as well as threats and intimidation. The cumulative effect of the ill-treatment on each child may, in some cases, amount to torture. As noted earlier, children are generally considered to be anyone under 18 years of age.

Ill-treatment begins at the moment of arrest, when many children are arrested during night-time raids on the family home, before being tied, often painfully so, and blindfolded. The destabilising effect of these night-time arrests is compounded by the fact that few children or parents are informed where the child is being taken.

Once arrested, the journey to an interrogation centre routinely involves further ill-treatment, either because of the way the child is restrained and positioned in the vehicle, or because of further physical violence or verbal abuse. The transfer process can take many hours and often includes intermediate stops at settlements or military bases where further ill-treatment is reported, including in some cases, prolonged exposure to the elements, and lack of water or access to toilets.

Child detainees continue to be questioned in the absence of their parents as no legal requirement exists under Israeli military law entitling a child to have a parent present during questioning or interrogation. Generally, child detainees do not meet with a lawyer until after the conclusion of interrogations and are not effectively informed of their right to silence.

DCI-Palestine is seriously concerned by the increasing use of solitary confinement on Palestinian children during 2012 and 2013, to focus on the most recent years for which we have data. At least 42 children were held in solitary confinement while being subjected to repeated and prolonged interrogations, with the apparent purpose of obtaining a confession. During these interrogations, children reported being forced to sit in a low metal chair secured to the floor of the room, with their hands and feet cuffed to the chair, often for several hours. DCI-Palestine can offer no explanation for the increase.

The affidavits and information collected by DCI-Palestine suggest that amendments to Israeli military law that established a juvenile military court, raised the age of majority from 16 to 18, and improved notification requirements upon arrest have had only a marginal impact on the situation facing Palestinian children prosecuted under Israeli military law. These amendments have done almost nothing to address the widespread and systematic ill-treatment of Palestinian children during arrest, transfer or interrogation.

Table 1 shows common violations raised in the affidavits collected during 2012 and 2013.

Complaints and areas of concern		West Bank			
		Number of cases	Percentage	Number of cases	Percentage
		2012		2013	
	Total affidavits collected	108	100.0%	98	
1	Hand ties	105	97.2%	98	100.0%
2	No lawyer present during interrogation	107	99.1%	94	95.9%
3	Not informed of rights	103	95.4%	91	92.9%
4	Blindfolds	103	95.4%	92	93.9%
5	Not informed of reason for arrest	88	81.5%	96	98.0%
6	Physical violence	80	74.1%	75	76.5%
7	Verbal abuse, humiliation and intimidation	73	67.6%	73	74.5%
8	Strip searched	96	88.9%	78	79.6%
9	Denial of adequate food and water	88	81.5%	76	77.6%

10	Threats or inducement	61	56.5%	39	39.8%
11	Denial of access the toilet	72	66.7%	68	69.4%
12	Night arrest	49	45.4%	55	56.1%
13	Position abuse	45	41.7%	32	32.7%
14	Transfer on vehicle floor	49	45.4%	49	50.0%
15	Shown or signed paper in Hebrew	17	15.7%	21	21.4%
16	Solitary confinement for more than two days	19	17.6%	21	21.4%
17	Detained with adults	8	7.4%	3	3.1%
18	Attempted recruitment	4	3.7%	0	0.0%
19	Threat of sexual assault	2	1.9%	2	2.0%

Overview

Each year approximately 500-700 Palestinian children from the occupied West Bank are prosecuted in Israeli military courts after being arrested, interrogated and detained by the Israeli army, police and security agents.[1] Since 2000, around 8,000 Palestinian children have been detained and prosecuted in the Israeli military court system. This report focuses on information and data collected during 2012 and 2013 involving torture and other cruel, inhuman or degrading treatment or punishment (torture and ill-treatment) within the system, which generally occurs during the first 48 hours after an arrest.

Children are frequently arrested from the family home by heavily armed soldiers in the middle of the night. They are painfully tied and blindfolded before being placed in the back of a military vehicle and transferred to an interrogation and detention centre. It is rare for a child, or his/her parents to be told the reason for arrest, or where the child is being taken. The arrest and transfer process is frequently accompanied by both physical and verbal abuse.

On arrival at the interrogation and detention centre, the child is questioned in the absence of a lawyer or family member, and there is generally no provision for the audio-visual recording of the interrogation as a means of

1. Exact figures on the number of Palestinian children detained each year by Israeli authorities are not published by the Israel Prison Service (IPS). The estimate of 500-700 children is based on figures provided by the IPS of the number children in prison facilities at the end of each month, and the best estimate of DCI-Palestine lawyers who appear daily in the military courts and conduct regular prison visits.

independent oversight. Few children are informed of their right to silence. Children are frequently threatened and physically assaulted during interrogation often resulting in the provision of a coerced confession, or the signing of documents which the child is not given a chance to read or understand. In 15.7 percent of cases in 2012 and 21.4 percent of cases in 2013, children were shown or signed a statement in Hebrew, a language they do not understand.

Following interrogation, children are brought before a military court which has jurisdiction over children as young as 12 years old.[2] In the overwhelming majority of cases bail is denied and an order for detention until the end of the legal process will be made. Most children plead guilty, whether the offence was committed or not, as this is the quickest way out of the system.

During 2012 and 2013, DCI-Palestine dealt with 287 total cases involving child prisoners. Of these cases, DCI-Palestine referred a total of 47 cases to other lawyers. Out of the remaining 240 children that DCI represented in Israeli military courts, 181 children (73.2 percent) were charged and 60 children (25 percent) were not prosecuted in the military court system. Of the 181 children who were charged, 180 children (99.5 percent) were convicted including 38 children (21 percent) released on bail. Only 3 children (1.7 percent) that faced charges were acquitted.

Around 60 percent of Palestinian child prisoners are held at prisons and detention facilities inside Israel in violation of Article 76 of the Fourth Geneva Convention, which prohibits transfers out of an occupied territory. The practical consequences of this violation is that many children receive infrequent, or no family visits, due to the length of time it takes to obtain a permit, or because permits are denied for unspecified "security" reasons. Further, Palestinian children are not permitted use the telephone while in detention.

Recent Developments

Military Order 1711

Military Order 1711 came into effect in April 2013, reducing the maximum time a Palestinian child can be detained by Israeli authorities prior to appearing before a military court judge for the first time. The new order

---

2. Military Order 1651, §§ 1 and 191.

shortened the time from four days to 24 or 48 hours depending on a child's age. Children aged 12 to 13 must appear before a military court judge within 24 hours after their arrest, while the period is 48 hours for children aged 14 to 15.

Military Order 1711 does not alter the period for children aged 16 to 17 years, which remains 96 hours, the same time period applied to adult detainees. In all instances, this time period can be extended for additional 24, 48 or 96 hours for interrogation purposes.

Military juvenile court

Military Order 1644 established military juvenile courts in September 2009 to prosecute persons aged 12 to 17 years. Under the provision, children should be tried separately from adults, and after indictment the court can direct that a social welfare report be prepared on the child. However, in practice the juvenile military courts use the same facilities and court staff as the adult military courts.

While the establishment of a juvenile military court and amendments to Israeli military law have resulted in minimal changes to legal proceedings involving children, there has been no practical impact on the ill-treatment of Palestinian children during the first 48 hours after an arrest.

Significantly, under the new order, bail applications and hearings to determine whether a child remains in detention pending the conclusion of the case can still be heard by adult military courts, where judges have not necessarily received training to handle cases involving children. Further, the new order makes no changes to the time period during which a child can be denied access to a lawyer and does not impose specific guidelines relating to the release of children on bail – both of which are governed by the same provisions that apply to adults. Finally, the new order does not introduce any new guidelines specifically addressing the special needs of children when it comes to sentencing.

According to a report published by the Israeli organisation B'Tselem, there are few improvements in the situation facing children prosecuted in the military courts since the introduction of the military juvenile court, as the following extract highlights:

The rights of Palestinian minors are flagrantly violated at every stage of the proceedings conducted against them, from the initial arrest and removal from their homes, through interrogation and trial, to serving the prison sentence, and then release [...] The amendments to the military legislation are marginal and have failed to bring about meaningful change in the military system's treatment of minors.

Raising the age of majority

Military Order 1676 changed the age of majority in the military courts from 16 to 18 years for certain specific provisions. In practice, the amendment makes little substantive difference in the treatment of 16- and 17-year-old children. Importantly, the amendment does not apply to sentencing provisions. While the juvenile military court has jurisdiction over children aged 16 to 17 years, they remain subject to adult sentencing provisions under Israeli military law.

Notifying parents of arrest

Military Order 1676 includes a provision requiring that the parents of a detained child be notified of the arrest or detention. Importantly, the notification provision only applies to Israeli police and not the Israeli army, which conducts arrests in the West Bank. After an arrest, a child is in the custody of the Israeli army for several hours and sometimes days before they are transferred to police custody. Once in police custody, police officers must inform a child's parent that they have been detained as soon as possible after the child arrives at the police station. However, during an investigation and if not formally arrested, notification can be delayed for up to eight hours.

Notifying a lawyer of arrest

Military Order 1676 includes a provision whereby child detainees are to be informed that they have the right to consult with an attorney in private. Prior to commencing the investigation, the police must also contact the lawyer named by the child, provided that this does not delay the investigation.[3] Since the introduction of this provision in September 2011, DCI-Palestine

---

3. Military Order 1651, § 136(a) (as amended by Military Order 1676).

has not documented a single case in which a child has consulted privately with an attorney either before or during an interrogation.

Number of Palestinian Children in Detention

The average number of Palestinian children in Israeli military detention at the end of each month during 2012 was 198 and 199 during 2013. The data below is compiled by DCI-Palestine from information obtained from the Israeli Prison Service (IPS) and from Israeli army temporary detention facilities. The figures are not cumulative, but a snapshot of the number of children in detention at the end of each month.

Table 2: Total number of Palestinian children in Israeli detention at the end of each month												
	Jan	Feb	Mar	Apr	May	Jun	Jul	Aug	Sep	Oct	Nov	Dec	Aver.
2009	389	423	420	391	346	355	342	339	326	325	306	305	355
2010	318	343	342	335	305	291	284	286	269	256	228	213	289
2011	222	221	226	220	211	209	202	180	164	150	161	135	192
2012	170	187	206	220	234	221	211	195	189	164	178	195	198
2013	223	236	238	238	223	193	195	179	179	159	173	154	199

During 2012, an average of 29 children between 12 and 15 years old were in Israeli military detention at the end of each month.

Table 3: Number of young (12-15) Palestinians in Israeli detention at the end of each month												
	Jan	Feb	Mar	Apr	May	Jun	Jul	Aug	Sep	Oct	Nov	Dec	Aver.
2009	50	54	53	47	39	47	42	39	40	44	41	42	44
2010	44	41	39	32	25	23	18	20	32	34	32	30	31
2011	34	45	45	37	38	38	40	34	35	30	33	19	36
2012	26	24	31	33	39	35	34	30	28	21	21	23	29
2013	31	39	39	44	48	41	35	30	27	15	16	14	32

During 2012 and 2013, no administrative detention orders were issued for anyone under 18 years old. However, DCI-Palestine continues to recommend that no child should be the subject of administrative detention and Israeli military law should be amended to reflect this position.

Specific Areas of Concern

Young children (12-15 years) in detention

DCI-Palestine remains concerned at the number of young children (12-15 years) being arrested, prosecuted and detained in the Israeli military court system. In 2012 and 2013, 30 percent of child prisoners were between 12 and 15. Israel has ratified the UN Convention on the Right of the Child which provides that the 'arrest, detention or imprisonment of a child ... shall be used only as a measure of last resort and for the shortest appropriate period of time.'[4] Alternatives to detention should be found for these young children.

Confessional evidence

In 75.2 percent of cases documented by DCI-Palestine in 2012 and 2013, children provided a confession during a coercive interrogation and in 18.4 percent of cases, the confession was written in the Hebrew language. These interrogations take place in the absence of a lawyer and/or family member, and are not audio-visually recorded. It is these confessions that then form the primary evidence against the child in the military courts.

Bail

Out of 181 cases charged from the files that DCI-Palestine represented in 2012 and 2013 just 38 were released on bail, which means that Palestinian children in the military courts were released on bail in just 15.7 percent of cases; to put it another way, in 84.3 percent of cases before the Israeli military courts, the child was kept in pre-trial detention. This would appear to be contrary to well-established and legally binding principles of juvenile justice whereby incarceration should be a measure of last resort.[5]

---

4. UN Convention on the Rights of the Child – Article 37(b).
5. See Article 37(b) of the Convention on the Rights of the Child (1989) (ratified by the State party in 1991).

Independent and impartial tribunal

It is questionable whether the use of military courts to try civilians can ever satisfy the requirements under international human rights law to a trial before an independent and impartial tribunal, as the judges are all serving officers subject to military discipline and dependent on superiors for promotion.[6]

Impunity

In 2013 DCI-Palestine submitted a total of 15 complaints over the alleged ill-treatment and torture of Palestinian children by Israeli soldiers and police. In thirteen of the cases, Israeli authorities failed to notify DCI-Palestine whether they had opened an investigation. The remaining two cases resulted in the military advocate general's decision to close the investigation due to insufficient evidence. Israeli authorities deem the refusal of victims to testify without the presence of a lawyer as insufficient evidence.

Since 2000, Yesh Din, an Israeli human rights group, reports that only five percent of complaints submitted to the Military Police Criminal Investigations Division have led to an indictment. Israel's poor record of accountability, in practice, sends a loud message that grave human rights violations against Palestinians can be committed with total impunity.

Detention inside Israel

In the Israeli military court system, Palestinian child detainees are initially held at Israeli military interrogation centres and police stations, generally in the West Bank, before being transferred to Israeli prisons operated by the Israeli Prison Service (IPS). Children are detained in interrogation centres for anywhere between several hours to several months, before being transferred to IPS operated facilities. All but one of the IPS facilities used to detain Palestinian children are located inside Israel, in contravention of Article 76 of the Fourth Geneva convention.

---

6. See UN Human Rights Committee, General Comment No. 32 – Article 14: *Right to equality before courts and tribunals and to a fair trial*, UN Doc: CCPR/C/GC/32, 23 August 2007, page 6, paragraph 22. See also Sharon Weill, "The judicial arm of the occupation: the Israeli military courts in the occupied territories," *International Review of the Red Cross*, Volume 89, Number 866, June 2007, pages 399 to 400.

Torture and ill-treatment

Palestinian children are often arrested at checkpoints, off the street or most commonly, from the family home. In the case of house arrests, large numbers of Israeli soldiers typically surround the family home in the early hours of the morning. Once a child has been identified for arrest s/he is often beaten or kicked before being blindfolded with his/her hands tied behind his/her back with plastic ties. The child will then be placed into the back of a military vehicle where s/he usually suffers further physical and psychological abuse on the way to the interrogation and detention centre. Upon arrest, children and their families are seldom informed of the charges against them.

On arrival at the interrogation and detention centre the child is either placed in a cell or taken straight for interrogation. Common interrogation practices include beating, kicking, verbal abuse and threats. The child is often threatened with long term detention if s/he does not confess or threats are made against the child's family.

In most cases the child confesses to the allegations put to him within the first two hours of interrogation. It is not uncommon for the child to be given a confession written in Hebrew to sign, a language few Palestinian children understand.[7]

Fair trial rights

In 77 percent of cases documented by DCI-Palestine in 2012 and 2013, children provided a confession during a coercive interrogation and in 18.4 percent of cases, the confession was written in the Hebrew language. These interrogations take place in the absence of a lawyer and/or family member, and are not audio-visually recorded. It is these confessions that then form the primary evidence against the child in the military courts.

The following sections are based on an analysis of the 206 affidavits collected by DCI-Palestine in 2012 and 2013 from children in the Israeli military detention system. The affidavits detail what children experience during the arrest, transfer and interrogation phases, as well as prosecution in a military court and imprisonment. This section is not an exhaustive list, but the issues repeatedly raised by children in their affidavits.

---

7. For further information see a report by DCI-Palestine - Palestinian Child Prisoners: The systematic and institutionalized ill-treatment and torture of Palestinian children by Israeli authorities (June 2009), pages 21 to 24.

In assessing the gravity of the ill-treatment reported by the children in their testimonies, it is important to consider the totality of the evidence from the moment of arrest to their appearance in a military court, as well considering their age, physical and psychological development and relative position of inferiority.

It should be noted that in all 206 cases, children experienced multiple forms of ill-treatment, not just a single, isolated incident. This is important in assessing the gravity of ill-treatment, as the cumulative effect must be taken into consideration, rather than viewing each individual act in isolation. When the totality of the evidence is considered, a pattern of systematic ill-treatment emerges, much of which amounts to cruel, inhuman or degrading treatment or punishment, for the purposes of the UN Convention against Torture, and in some cases, torture–both of which are absolutely prohibited.[8]

Arrested between midnight and 5 a.m.

In 104 out of 206 cases (50.5 percent), children report being arrested from their homes between midnight and 5 a.m. Many children report waking up to the sound of heavily-armed Israeli soldiers banging on their front door and shouting instructions to the family to leave the house. The practice of arresting children during night raids can lead to a lasting sense of insecurity.

There are no specific guarantees or safeguards under international law that specifically regulate the times at which a child can be arrested. However, Israeli civilian law restricts the times at which children can be interrogated which in practice influences the times at which Israeli children are arrested.[9] No such provision is included in Israeli military law, which applies to Palestinian children in the West Bank.

A practical alternative to arresting children at night is to issue a summons to appear at a police station during daylight hours. This procedure has been successfully employed by Israeli authorities in a limited number of cases, and would give effect to the guiding legal principle that the best interests of the child should be a primary consideration.[10]

---

8. The State of Israel ratified the UN Convention against Torture and Other Cruel, Inhuman or Degrading Treatment or Punishment in 1991, and is legally bound by its terms.
9. Israel Youth Law, § 9(J).
10. UN Convention on the Rights of the Child, Art. 3

Hand ties and blindfolds

In 203 out of 206 cases (98.5 percent), children had their hands bound, and in 195 out of 206 cases (94.7 percent), the children were also blindfolded. These figures remain little changed from affidavits and evidence gathered by DCI-Palestine during 2011. The most common method of restraining a child is by tying his hands behind his back with a single plastic tie. Many children experience pain in their hands and wrists as a result of these ties, which can remain on for several hours during arrest, transfer and interrogation. In some cases blood circulation is affected because ties are very tight, causing their hands to swell and turn blue.

In April 2010, new procedures for tying detainees were introduced by the Israeli army. The new procedures stated that hands should be tied from the front, unless security considerations require tying from behind; three plastic ties should be used, one around each wrist, and one connecting the two; there should be the space of a finger between the ties and the wrist; and the restraints should avoid causing suffering as much as possible.

In the overwhelming majority of cases documented by DCI-Palestine, the April 2010 procedures are not implemented in any regard as children's hands continue to be tied with a single tie behind their back.

Transferred on floor of vehicle

In 98 out of 206 cases (47.6 percent), children reported being placed on the metal floor of a military vehicle for the duration of the journey from their home to an interrogation centre, which can take several hours. Often, Israeli soldiers will be sitting on benches on either side of the child and subjecting him to physical violence and verbal abuse.

Physical violence and verbal abuse

In 155 out of 206 cases (75.2 percent), children reported being subjected to some form of physical violence during their arrest, transfer or interrogation. In most cases, physical violence against child detainees such as slapping, punching and kicking occurs while the child is bound and blindfolded.

In some cases, Israel soldiers use excessive force against Palestinian children when conducting arrests near checkpoints, settlements and roads used by soldiers or settlers. Arrests outside the context of a night raid tend to involve more severe physical violence such as being hit with the stock of a rifle or with a soldier's helmet.

During interrogation, children are led into a room still tied and blindfolded and forced to sit in a chair. In some cases, children remained tied for the duration of the interrogation, which can last for several hours. Children held in solitary confinement for interrogation purposes are usually tied to a low metal chair in the centre of the room. Physical violence against children during interrogation reportedly includes pushing, slapping and kicking.

In 146 out of 206 cases (70.9 percent), children reported some form of verbal abuse, intimidation or humiliating treatment during their arrest, transfer or subsequent interrogation.

Threats

In 100 out of 206 cases (48.5 percent), children reported being threatened by their interrogator. Interrogations involve a combination of physical violence, threats and verbal abuse. The prohibition against torture and ill-treatment also covers acts that cause mental suffering, such as intimidation and threats. As with physical forms of torture and ill-treatment, the victim's age and position of inferiority must be taken into account when assessing psychological forms of ill-treatment. Repeated threats and constant shouting are common during an interrogation.

The types of threats reported include threats of physical violence, long-term imprisonment, sexual assault, solitary confinement, death threats and unspecified threats, all of which are apparently aimed at obtaining a confession.

Solitary confinement

In 42 out of 206 cases (20.4 percent), solitary confinement was used on children in Israeli military detention. In the overwhelming majority of cases, children are held in solitary confinement while being subjected to repeated and prolonged interrogations, with the apparent purpose of obtaining a confession. During these interrogations, children report being forced to sit in a low metal chair secured to the floor of the room, with their hands and feet cuffed to the chair, often for several hours.

Children held in solitary confinement at Al Jalame interrogation and detention centre report being detained in a tiny cell with a toilet and a concrete bed, or a thin, dirty mattress. Meals, sometimes inedible, are passed to children through a flap in the door, and there are no windows. The only source of light comes from a dim yellow bulb that is reported to be kept on 24 hours a day.

The detrimental psychological and physical effects of detaining persons in solitary confinement are well documented and include panic attacks, fear of impending death, depression, social withdrawal, hopelessness, unprovoked anger, short attention span, disorientation, paranoia, psychotic episodes, self-mutilation, and attempted suicide.

For these reasons, UN Special Rapporteur on Torture Juan Méndez called for a complete ban on the use of solitary confinement for children in a report submitted to the UN General Assembly in 2011. He concluded that the use of solitary confinement "can amount to torture or cruel, inhuman or degrading treatment or punishment, during pre-trial detention, indefinitely or for a prolonged period, for persons with mental disabilities or juveniles."

DCI-Palestine maintains that the practice of using solitary confinement on children in Israeli detention facilities must be stopped immediately, and the prohibition must be enshrined in law.

Strip searches

In 174 out of 206 cases (84.5 percent), children reported being strip-searched at least once shortly after their arrest and detention in the Israeli military court system. The majority of children describe feelings of embarrassment, shame and humiliation as a result.

Confessions and documentation written in Hebrew

In 38 out of 206 cases (18.4 percent), children reported being shown, or forced to sign, documentation written in Hebrew, a language the overwhelming majority of Palestinian children do not understand. These documents are then included in court files, which are in the possession of both the military prosecutors and judges, neither of who express criticism or surprise regarding this practice.[11]

---

11. Pursuant to Article 147 of the Fourth Geneva Convention, wilfully depriving a protected person of the rights of a fair and regular trial is a grave breach of the Convention and attracts personal criminal responsibility. Further, under Article 146, all parties to the Convention have a positive legal obligation to search out and prosecute those responsible for grave breaches.

Detention inside Israel in violation of the Fourth Geneva Convention

Around 60 percent of Palestinian children in the Israeli military detention system are held in facilities located inside Israel in violation of Article 76 of the Fourth Geneva Convention, which prohibits the transfer of prisoners out of occupied territory.[12] The practical consequences of this violation is that many children receive either limited or no family visits due to freedom of movement restrictions and time necessary to obtain a permit to visit a prison.

Failure to exclude evidence obtained by coercion or force

According to DCI-Palestine lawyers that represent children in Israeli military courts, evidence is rarely excluded that is obtained through force or coercion.

DCI-Palestine maintains that Israeli military courts must exclude all evidence obtained by force or coercion during an interrogation, as well as when a child is not appropriately informed of his right to silence.

Presence of a lawyer or family member during interrogation

In 201 of 206 cases (97.6 percent), children were interrogated without the presence of a lawyer or family member. Aside from the right to access legal counsel and have a parent present during interrogation under international human rights law,[13] the presence of a third-party can be an effective measure to limit the use of torture, ill-treatment and other coercive techniques during questioning.

Israeli children, including those residing in settlements in the occupied West Bank and East Jerusalem, generally have the right to have a parent present during interrogation.[14] Although no such right is granted to Palestinian children under Israeli military law, the President of the Military Court of Appeals has previously stated that the "spirit" of the Youth Law also applies to Palestinian children living in occupied territory.[15]

---

12. Fourth Geneva Convention, Art. 76 states "Protected persons accused of offences shall be detained in the occupied country, and if convicted they shall serve their sentences therein."

13. Convention on the Rights of the Child, Art. 40(2)(b)(ii) and (iv).

14. Youth Law, § 9(H) (1971).

15. Mil. Ct. App. (Judea and Samaria) 2912/09, Military Prosecutor v N.A.

Impunity for Violations

Many Palestinian families refuse to file complaints alleging mistreatment against Israeli authorities for fear of retaliation, or simply because they do not believe the system is fair or impartial. In 2012, DCI-Palestine filed eight complaints with Israeli authorities concerning the ill-treatment and torture of children while in Israeli military detention. In 2013, DCI-Palestine filed 15 complaints on behalf of ten children. The results of these complaints are presented below:

Table 4: Complaints submitted by DCI-Palestine on behalf of child detainees in 2012 and 2013					
#	Name	Age	Details	Date of complaint	Status
1	Rasheed J.	16	On 4 November 2011, Rasheed was arrested by Israeli soldiers and transferred to the Al Jalame facility, inside Israel. He reports being held in solitary confinement in a windowless cell for 13 days and being repeatedly interrogated whilst tied to a chair.	14 Feb 2012	Opened
2	Mahmoud S.	17	On 10 March 2012, Mahmoud was arrested by Israeli soldiers when he was walking beside a road near the village of Azzun, where he lives. He reports being ill-treated during the process of arrest, transfer and interrogation.	9 May 2012	Opened
3	Mohammad H.	14	On 15 March 2012, Mohammad H. was arrested from his family home in East Jerusalem at 4:00 am. He reports being ill-treated during the process of arrest, transfer and interrogation by the Israeli authorities.	16 May 2012	Opened

Table 4: Complaints submitted by DCI-Palestine on behalf of child detainees in 2012 and 2013					
#	Name	Age	Details	Date of complaint	Status
4	Sadem D.	16	On 16 March 2012, Sadem D. was arrested while he was grazing sheep with two other boys near the village of Fasayil, in the Jordan Valley. He reports being beaten and remaining tied for 19 hours.	17 May 2012	Opened
5	'Ala H.	15	On 10 May 2012, 'Ala and two of his friends were arrested by Israeli soldiers as they walked to see a friend in a neighbouring village. They were accused of throwing stones at settler cars and report being repeatedly beaten by the soldiers.	26 May 2012	Unknown
6	Mohammad J.	16	On 10 May 2012, Mohammad and two of his friends were arrested by Israeli soldiers as they walked to see a friend in a neighbouring village. They were accused of throwing stones at settler cars and report being repeatedly beaten by the soldiers.	26 May 2012	Opened
7	Mohammad E.	16	On 6 June 2012, Mohammad E. was arrested by Israeli soldiers at 4:00 am, and held in solitary confinement for 12 days in Al Jalame interrogation centre.	16 Jul 2012	Opened
8	Hammam N.	16	On 18 June 2012, Hammam was arrested by Israeli soldiers at night. He reports being ill-treated during the process of arrest, transfer and interrogation.	10 Aug 2012	Unknown

Table 4: Complaints submitted by DCI-Palestine on behalf of child detainees in 2012 and 2013					
#	Name	Age	Details	Date of complaint	Status
9	Suleiman K.	17	On 25 October 2012, Suleiman was arrested by Israeli soldiers at 4:00 am, and held in solitary confinement for 18 days in Al Jalame interrogation centre.	12 Jan 2013	Unknown
10	Jamal S.	16	On 22 October 2012, Jamal was arrested by Israeli soldiers at 2:00 am, and held in solitary confinement for 4 days in Al Jalame interrogation centre.	12 Jan 2013	Unknown
11	Adham D.	16	On 14 October 2012, Adham was arrested by Israeli soldiers, and held in solitary confinement for 12 days in Al Jalame interrogation centre.	12 Jan 2013	Unknown
12	Abdullah S.	16	On 27 September 2012, Abdullah was arrested by Israeli soldiers at 2:00 am, and held in solitary confinement for 6 days in Al Jalame interrogation centre.	12 Jan 2013	Unknown
13	Mujahed S.	17	On 24 September 2012, Mujahed was arrested by Israeli soldiers at 12:00 am, and held in solitary confinement for 29 days in Al Jalame interrogation centre.	12 Jan 2013	Unknown
14	Majd H.	16	On 9 February 2013, Majd was arrested by Israeli soldiers at 3:00 a.m. from his home and was subjected to physical violence during interrogation. He was forced to clean bathrooms and rooms at Huwara interrogation and detention centre.	26 Feb 2013	Closed

Table 4: Complaints submitted by DCI-Palestine on behalf of child detainees in 2012 and 2013					
#	Name	Age	Details	Date of complaint	Status
15	Hendi S.	16	On 9 February 2013, Hendi was arrested by Israeli soldiers at 3:00 am from his home and was subjected to verbal threats and abuse of a sexual nature. He was forced to clean bathrooms and rooms at Huwara interrogation and detention centre.	26 Feb 2013	Unknown
16	Mohammad A.	15	On 10 September 2013, Mohammad was arrested by Israeli soldiers arrested at 1:00 pm near the separation wall. He was beat by soldiers during arrest and transfer.	27 Nov 2013	Unknown
17	Ali S.	14	On 12 September 2013, Ali was arrested by Israeli soldiers after being stopped and physical assaulted by an Israeli settler driving by on a nearby road. Israeli soldiers beat Ali during arrest and transfer, and later extinguished a cigarette on his lip.	27 Nov 2013	Unknown
18	Hendi S.	17	On 19 September 2013, Hendi was arrested from his home at 2:30 am by Israeli soldiers. Hendi was subjected to physical violence during arrest, transfer and was beaten just prior to interrogation.	27 Nov 2013	Unknown

Concluding Remarks

The affidavits collected by DCI-Palestine during 2012 and 2013 indicate that the ill-treatment of Palestinian children held in Israeli military detention is widespread and systematic. The cumulative effect of the ill-treatment experienced by all of the children must also be considered when assessing its gravity. In some cases this cumulative effect, coupled with the child's age, may result in the treatment being properly categorised as torture. It is important to note however, that both ill-treatment and torture are absolutely prohibited and criminalised under international law.

Most children held in the Israeli military detention system are arrested from villages located close to friction points, namely settlements built in violation of international law, and roads used by the Israeli army or settlers.

Recent amendments to the military orders relating to children have had little impact whatsoever on their treatment during the critical first 48 hours after an arrest, where most of the ill-treatment occurs at the hands of soldiers, policemen and interrogators.

Recommendations

1. No child should be prosecuted in military courts which lack comprehensive fair trial and juvenile justice standards. DCI-Palestine recommends that as a minimum safeguard in the light of consistent reports of torture and ill-treatment, the following:

2. Except in extreme and unusual circumstances, all arrests of children should occur during daylight hours;

3. In all cases the use of single plastic hand ties and blindfolds should be prohibited and the prohibition must be effectively enforced;

4. All children must have access to a lawyer of their choice prior to interrogation, and through the interrogation process;

5. All children must be entitled to have a parent present at all times during their interrogation;

6. In every case the interrogation of children should be audio-visually recorded;

7. In all cases evidence obtained as a result of torture or ill-treatment must be excluded by the military courts;

8. In all cases where incriminating evidence is obtained during interrogation when the child was not appropriately informed of his/her right to silence, this evidence must be excluded by the military courts;

9. The practice of using solitary confinement and administrative detention orders on children in Israeli military detention must be stopped immediately, and the prohibition must be enshrined in law;

10. Effective accountability measures must be introduced to ensure all credible reports of torture and ill-treatment are properly investigated in accordance with international standards and that perpetrators are brought to justice.

Five Case Stories

Ahmad A. (17)

Detained: 7 April 2014
Location: Osarin, Nablus
Ill-treatment, torture, coerced confession, unlawful transfer

Ahmad A., 17, was arrested on charges of throwing stones. On 6 April, Ahmad's father received a telephone call requesting that his son, Ahmad, report to Huwara District Coordination Office (DCO) the next morning. No reason was provided by the Israeli intelligence officer. On 7 April, Ahmad and his father arrived at Huwara DCO around 10 a.m. His father was held outside while Ahmad was directed within and strip searched. Ahmad recounts, "While he was searching me, he pushed me against the wall and called me a 'son of a whore.'"

An Israeli intelligence officer instructed him that he was under arrest without stating charges. Ahmad was bound, blindfolded and detained in a room for about thirty minutes. Soldiers then forced Ahmad to walk—punching and kicking his back and legs—to Huwara Interrogation and Detention Center (IDC).

In the course of detention, Ahmad was verbally and physically assaulted by soldiers multiple times. One assault caused his ear to bleed and impaired hearing. Ahmad notes that he did not receive any medical attention for this injury—nor food or water—until he arrived at Megiddo Prison, around 5 p.m.

On 8 April, Ahmad was interrogated for approximately four hours in Salem IDC without the presence of a lawyer, family member or any explanation of his rights. He was slapped and hit on the head during interrogation, while still shackled. Ahmad signed a confession in Arabic after reading it. He first appeared before a judge on 10 April 2014.

Basheer D. (17)
Detained: 4 February 2014
Location: Beita, Nablus
Ill-treatment, torture, unlawful transfer

Israeli forces took Basheer, 17, into custody when he reported to an Israeli interrogation center for questioning as demanded the day before by an Israeli intelligence officer via mobile phone.

On 3 February, Basheer received a call on his mobile phone from an Israeli intelligence officer demanding that he present himself the next day at Huwara District Coordination Office for questioning at 9 am. He reported for questioning on 4 February and, without being informed of any charges against him, he was arrested and told he would be sent to interrogation. Basheer was promptly bound and blindfolded and taken to Huwara Interrogation and Detention Center, where he was strip-searched and detained until 8 p.m. He was then transferred to Megiddo prison inside Israel, arriving around 11 p.m.

On 6 February, Basheer was brought to Salem Interrogation and Detention Center for interrogation. With no access to an attorney and no family member present, an Israeli interrogator accused Basheer of throwing stones and Molotov cocktails. He then told Basheer that other children had provided statements against him. After denying the accusations and refusing to confess, Basheer was called a liar, kicked on his legs, and punched in the stomach and head. "I became very scared of him and decided to confess," says Basheer. "Others had already said things about me, so I confessed to throwing stones and Molotov cocktails at Israeli cars."

Basheer appeared the first time before a military court judge at Salem military court following his interrogation.

Amr J. (17)

Detained: 20 November 2013
Location: Al-Arroub refugee camp, Hebron
Night arrest, ill-treatment, coerced confession, signed papers in Hebrew

Israeli soldiers arrested Amr, 17, from his home in the middle of the night and accused him of throwing stones. Around 3:30 a.m., Amr told DCI-Palestine he woke to banging on the front door of his home. About 15 Israeli soldiers stormed the house and one soldier asked specifically for him. When Amr identified himself, the soldier tied Amr's hands behind his back with a single plastic cord and dragged him out of the house. Amr was placed in a military truck, blindfolded and forced to kneel on the metal floor.

During transfer to Etzion interrogation and detention center, he was kicked and punched all over his torso. About an hour later he started shaking and collapsed to the ground. A military doctor was called, but did not provide him with any medical treatment. Shortly after, he was transferred to an interrogation facility, where he was not allowed to consult with an attorney and was subject to prolonged interrogations by three different interrogators.

"[The third interrogator] was in his early forties, bald and tall," says Amr. "He made the same accusations and said he would not leave me until I confessed. About 15 minutes later, I decided to confess because I was really tired and in bad shape." The interrogator made Amr sign a confession drafted in Hebrew, and he was transferred that evening to Ofer prison near Ramallah. Around 5 p.m. the next day, Amr appeared in Ofer military court. He was represented by a DCI-Palestine lawyer and released on 1,000 NIS ($290 USD) bail.

Tareq E. (9)

Detained: 15 November 2013
Location: Kafr Qaddum, Qalqilya
Detained while under the age of criminal responsibility, ill-treatment

Israeli soldiers detained Tareq, 9, prior to a weekly demonstration demanding that Israeli forces reopen the main road in the village of Kafr Qaddum.

Around 8 a.m., Tareq told DCI-Palestine that he and a few other young boys from the village wandered toward where the protest would start that day. On the main street, Tareq saw several tires on fire. They approached and threw stones at the burning tires. Suddenly, four Israeli soldiers rushed toward the boys. "I looked behind me and saw four Israeli soldiers jumping off the retaining wall near the street and rushing toward us," says Tareq. "They were hiding there, so we all started running north toward the mountain. As we started running, a stun grenade landed two meters (six feet) ahead of us, and we all stopped."

A soldier grabbed Tareq and tied his hands behind his back with a single plastic cord. Crying and scared, Tareq and the others were forced to walk 100 meters (330 feet) toward the Israeli settlement at the end of the road. When they arrived at the front gate an Israeli soldier sitting in a military jeep shouted at the boys in Arabic, questioning them about the burning tires. After a short period, Tareq and the others were untied and released.

Wasim N. (16)
Detained: 18 October 2013
Location: Beita, Nablus
Night arrest, ill-treatment, solitary confinement, unlawful transfer

Israeli soldiers arrested Wasim, 16, from his home in the middle of the night and accused him of throwing stones and Molotov cocktails.

Around 2 a.m., Israeli soldiers approached Wasim's home, banged on the door and entered. A soldier grabbed Wasim's shirt, dragged him into the staircase, and asked for his ID. When Wasim's uncle asked the soldiers why he was being arrested, they pointed their rifles at him and ordered him to step away. Wasim was quickly forced down the stairs by the soldiers. "Other soldiers were at the end of the stairway," says Wasim. "One of them wrapped his arm around my neck and started squeezing really hard. I felt so much pain as if I was choking. I shouted in pain and felt like my head was about to explode."

His hands were tied behind his back with a single plastic cord and he was blindfolded before being put in the back of a military jeep. After being denied access to a toilet at Huwara interrogation and detention center, Wasim started to shiver, felt dizzy and then vomited. Three hours later he was transferred to Petah Tikva interrogation and detention center inside Israel, where he spent 14 days in solitary confinement for interrogation purposes.

6. Conscientious Objectors

New Profile is a feminist movement of women and men,[1] who know that we need not live in a soldiers' state. Israeli society is capable of a determined peace politics. It need not be a militarized society. We are convinced that we need not go on being endlessly recruited, need not go on living as soldiers. We wish to live in a civil society that fosters the values of tolerance and democracy and seeks peaceful solutions to its problems.

We realize that the words "national security" have often masked calculated decisions to choose military action for the achievement of political goals. We are unwilling to take part in such choices. We will not go on enabling them by obediently, uncritically supplying soldiers to the military which implements them. We will not go on being recruited, raising children for recruitment, supporting recruited family members, while those in charge of the country go on easily deploying the army, rather than building other solutions.

Expressing such opinions in Israel is difficult. In a soldiers' state there is a hierarchy of those who count and those who don't, a hierarchy shaped by the ideal of the male warrior, who, in the Israeli case, is also invariably Jewish. Military officers are held to have privileged knowledge, giving them precedence in decision making. Attitudes casting doubts on "security" related decisions, questioning the state's enormous military budgets, or its ongoing policies of military confrontation, are branded "naive," "hysterical," "ignorant." An attitude that dares question the fundamental principle of willingness to enlist into the military is still often rejected as illegitimate in Israel.

Our position—the supposedly "ignorant" position—aims to change the mindsets that have been perpetuating war in Israel for many decades. It is a position prioritizing life and the protection of life first and foremost. On this view, Israel's education system and much of its culture and media convey militarist messages. The content they instill in all of us prepares young people for enlistment as a self-obvious act and for unquestioning obedience.

---

1. All materials in this section are sourced from: http://www.newprofile.org/english/

They nurture admiration for might and physical prowess, an aggrandizement of the Jewish nation, and conversely, the devaluation of the lives of people of Arab and other nationalities. Every parent takes an active part in educating children to become soldiers. We are all accountable for this before them and before ourselves.

And yet, there are many women and men, parents and youngsters, who profoundly, morally object to Israel's continued wars of choice. We oppose the continued use of military means, including privatized security forces, to enforce Israeli rule beyond the Green Line. We oppose the use of the army, police, other security forces and private security firms in the ongoing oppression and discrimination of the Palestinian citizens of Israel, while demolishing their homes, denying them building and development rights, using violence to disperse their demonstrations.

Given this widespread opposition to the kind of roles assigned to the Israeli army, police, and other forces, for many years, many young women and men are currently avoiding conscription or avoiding combat duty. Some refuse for other reasons, such as objection to soldiering as such, a pacifist worldview, etc. Others still refuse for economic reasons—out of the need to support their families financially. About half of those subject to conscription under Israeli law do not in fact enlist, and many more terminate their military service early on in their term of duty. It is common knowledge that a large proportion of these in fact choose not to enlist. They feel unable to identify with the implications and meaning of military service in Israel today. Faced with no legal option for conscientious objection, a discharge on grounds of poor health is virtually their only way out. Opting out is even more widespread among reservists. According to some publications, only about one-sixth of Israel's potential reserves force, as the military itself defines it, perform active reserves service. We all know how pervasive this phenomenon is.

To date, Israeli law does not recognize the basic human right not to be a soldier. We regard the Israeli conscription law as discriminatory and non-democratic. For our part, we refuse to go on raising our children to see enlistment as a supreme and overriding value. We demand a fundamental change in the education system, so that it provides a truly democratic civic education, teaching the practice of peace and conflict resolution, rather than training children to enlist and accept warfare.

Recruitment and Refusal

In the face of a militaristic society which glorifies military service and idolizes conscription, each year tens of thousands of young men and women choose not to take part in the Israeli army. In fact, only about half of the eligible citizens enlist, and many more leave during their service. There are many reasons for this wide ranging phenomenon - economical, political, ideological, religious and medical reasons as well as a refusal to join an oppressive, chauvinistic and violent program. Military service is a burden on many (and an asset for a few) and refusal and avoidance of military service is a complicated issue, not as cut and dry as the media would portray it.

The counseling network for "refusers" and avoiders provides information and support for those who have decided not to enlist or to leave the army.

Militarism

Militarism is a prevalent ideology which upholds the military as sacred, an ideology which glorifies military values and the war ethos, irrespective of the actual state of security. In a militaristic society the military is revered, its leaders held in the highest regard, and in turn the military's norms and values pervade and dominate the civil society, in areas such as education, entertainment, urban space, social services, family life, etc.

The Jewish society in Israel perceives military action as normal, and wars as unavoidable. It is a society in which integration in society is conditioned on military service, which is framed as both a burden and a social duty one must not avoid. A society in whose towns and cities it is common to see armed soldiers roam the streets, where parks are decorated with war memorabilia and streets are commonly named after wars, battles, military units and generals; a society which views other nations as either for us or against us; a society in which women would never be full, equal members in the political process because they are excluded from positions of power within the military.

Youth

Our young people are expected to enlist together with the rest of their classmates, without understanding why they are drafted, without thinking about the possibility of not being drafted, and generally without asking questions.

The purpose of the New Profile youth groups is providing tools for critical thinking, to raise questions related to the everyday political reality, to think about social change, what it means and where all that meets us? In addition, the New Profile youth groups try to raise the questions that bother us. In the groups we talk about treatment to women in society and the army, animal rights, the occupation and the attitude towards Arabs in Israeli society, the social gaps in the country (in and outside the Army), the education system values which educates us all and every issue that members of the group raise.

The groups meet in Haifa, Jerusalem and Tel Aviv once a week and are facilitated by two members of New Profile.

Conscientious Objectors Currently in Israeli Military Prisons
(9 June 2014) Third Prison Term for Conscientious Objector Uriel Ferera

(30 April 2014) Seventh Prison Term for Conscientious Objector Omar Saad

(9 March 2014) Imprisonment of Conscientious Objector Mahmood Saad

New Profile's Networks and Communities
The refuser network in Israel
Yesh Gvul - www.yeshgvul.org

The Druze Initiative Committee

Shministim - www.december18th.org

Feminism
Kayan - www.kayan.org.il

Isha L'Isha - www.isha.org.il/eng/

Guns off the Kitchen Table - http://www.youtube.com/watch?v=zJfIgzB_A84http://on.fb.me/WONKhK

Anti-occupation and movements for social change

Combatants for Peace - www.cfpeace.org

Anarchists Against the Wall - www.awalls.org

Coalition of Women for Peace- www.coalitionofpeace.org

Machsom Watch - www.machsomwatch.org

Adrid - The National Committee for the Rights of the Internally Displaced in Israel - (You can read more about Adrid in this pdf file) http://www.new-profile.org/nakba/adrid.pdf

Women in Black - http://www.facebook.com/groups/105319716164100/ http://www.womeninblack.org

Sheikh Jarrah Solidarity Movement - www.en.justjlm.org

All for Peace Radio - www.allforpeace.org/eng/

Gush Shalom - www.gush-shalom.org

Committee Against House Demolitions, (ICAHD) - www.icahd.org

Breaking the Silence - www.breakingthesilence.org.il

Ta'ayush - www.taayush.org

B'tselem - www.btselem.org

Gisha - www.gisha.org

Hamoked - Center for the Defence of the Individual - www.hamoked.org

Women's Organization for Political Prisoners (WOFPP) - http://www.wofpp.org/english/home.html

Physicians for Human Rights - www.phr.org.il

The Public Committee Against Torture in Israel (PCATI) - www.stoptorture.org.il

Rabbis for Human Rights - rhr.org.il/eng

Reut Sadaka - www.reutsadaka.org

Yesh Din - www.yesh-din.org

Palestinian Israeli Bereaved Families for Peace - www.theparentscircle.orghttp://www.facebook.com/ParentsCircleFamiliesForum

Boycott from Within - www.boycottisrael.info

The Other Voice - http://www.othervoice.org/welcome-eng.htm

Association of the Forty - http://www.assoc40.org/en/

Bustan - https://www.bustan.org http://www.facebook.com/pages/Bustan/137998598052

Regional Council of Unrecognized Villages - http://rcuv.wordpress.com/

Tarabut - http://www.tarabut.info/en/home/

New Profile's international connections and networks

Refusers Solidarity Network (RSN) - www.refusersolidarity.net

War Resisters International (WRI) - www.wri-irg.org

Heks-Eper (Open Forum) - http://www.heks.ch/en/worldwide/palestineisrael/

Ecumenical Accompaniment Program in Palestine and Israel (EAPPI) - www.eappi.org

Women's Peacemakers Program - www.ifor.org/WPP/

International Fellowship of Reconciliation (IFOR) - www.ifor.org

Interfaith Peace Builders (IFPB) - www.ifpb.org

The Siraj Center - www.sirajcenter.org

Quaker Peace and Social Witness (QPSW) - http://www.quaker.org.uk/working-peace

QIAR in Ramallah (Quakers International Affairs Representative) - http://www.ramallahquakers.org

American Friends Service Committee (AFSC) - www.afsc.org

Quaker Service Norway - http://www.kveker.org/index_eng.htm

Quaker Council for European Affairs - www.qcea.org

Nobel Women's Initiative - www.nobelwomensinitiative.org

Olympia-Rafah Mural Project - www.olympiarafahmural.org

Committee on the Rights of the Child - http://www2.ohchr.org/english/bodies/crc/

Connection e.V. - www.connection-ev.de

Jewish Voice for Peace (JVP) - www.jewishvoiceforpeace.org

Jewish Peace Fellowship - http://www.jewishpeacefellowship.org/

Juedisches Forum fur Friedan - http://ww1.juedisches-forum.de/html/israel_initiatives.html

Resource Center for Non Violence (RCNV) - www.rcnv.org

Conscience and Peace Tax International (CPTI) - www.cpti.ws

Defense for Children International - www.defenceforchildren.org

Child Soldiers International - http://www.child-soldiers.org/home

Christian Peacekeeper Teams - www.cpt.org

European Bureau for Conscientious Objectors (EBCO) - www.ebco-beoc.org

International Action Network on Small Arms (IANSA) - www.iansa-women.org

Bread for the World - http://www.brot-fuer-die-welt.de/english/index.php

SIVMO - http://www.sivmo.nl/about-sivmo.html

Global Fund for Women - www.globalfundforwomen.org

Independent Jewish Voices Canada www.ijvcanada.org

Karibu Foundation www.karibu.no

Other organizations and sites we think you should know about
Code Pink - www.codepink.org

Jewish Peace Fellowship - www.jewishpeacefellowship.org

The Middle East Children's Alliance - www.mecaforpeace.org

Human Rights Watch (HRW),

Israel and the Occupied Territories - http://www.hrw.org/
middle-eastn-africa/israel-and-occupied-territories

Amnesty International, Israel and the Occupied Palestine Territories
-http://www.amnesty.org/en/region/israel-occupied-palestinian-territories

Neged Neshek - www.negedneshek.org

Disarm the Conflict - http://disarmtheconflict.wordpress.com/israeli-arms/

Recommended films that include scenes with New Profile *
Dreams Deferred: The Struggle for Peace and Justice in Israel and Palestine
http://www.supportisraelfreepalestine.org/documentary_site/documentary.
html

Vimeo http://vimeo.com/30499381 *

Occupation Has No Future - www.UpheavalProductions.com/
occupation-has-no-future

Suggested publications
The Kibush Magazine - www.kibush.co.il

The Alternative Information Center - http://www.alternativenews.org/
english/

The Palestine Israel Journal - www.pij.org

+972 Online Magazine - www.972mag.com

The Day in Palestine - www.theheadlines.org

Exhibition
http://www.newprofile.org/english/Exhibition

7. Organizations Working with Prisoners and Human Rights

"Hurryyat" The Center for Defense of Liberties and Civil Rights "Hurryyat" is a Palestinian non-governmental and independent organization that contributes to the protection of the Palestinian liberties, civil and political rights.

Hurryyat thrives to enhance the rule of law within the Palestinian society, and to provide legal, financial and psychological assistance to both the Palestinian prisoners detained in Israeli jails and their families. This is achieved on a human rights-based approach to accomplish the following objectives:

Activating the social involvement and participation of the Palestinian community in protecting the Palestinian civil and political rights.

Organizing systematic advocacy initiatives directed towards enhancing Palestinian prisoners' conditions.

Contributing towards the efforts aiming at influencing the decision-making process in ways that protects human, social and political rights of Palestinian prisoners in Israeli jails.

Core values that make up the platform of Hurryyat's work are based on voluntary spirit, equality, participation, social justice, gender sensitivity, transparency and commitment to social development and democracy.

http://www.hurryyat.net/en/

Addameer (*Arabic for "conscience"*) **Prisoner Support and Human Rights Association** is a Palestinian non-governmental, civil institution that works to support Palestinian political prisoners held in Israeli and Palestinian prisons. Established in 1992 by a group of activists interested in human rights, the center offers free legal aid to political prisoners, advocates their rights at the national and international level, and works to end torture and other violations of prisoners' rights through monitoring, legal procedures and solidarity campaigns.

The programs of Addameer

Legal Aid Unit: Since its founding, Addameer›s legal aid work has formed the backbone of the organization›s work, with Addameer›s lawyers providing free legal representation and advice to hundreds of Palestinian detainees and their families every year, and working on precedent-setting cases of torture, fair trials and other violations affecting political prisoners.

Documentation and Research Unit: Addameer documents violations committed against Palestinian detainees, monitors their detention conditions through regular prison visits, and collects detailed statistics and information on detainees, which serve as the basis for its annual and thematic publications.

Advocacy and Lobbying Unit: Addameer›s advocacy work is aimed primarily at the international community, with the unit publishing statements and urgent appeals on behalf of detainees, briefing international delegations and the media, and submitting reports and individual complaints to the United Nations, urging stakeholders to pressure Israel to change its policies. The unit also works towards building local, Arab and international solidarity campaigns to oppose arbitrary detention and torture while supporting the rights of Palestinian prisoners.

Training and Awareness Unit: Addameer raises local awareness of prisoners' rights on three levels: by training Palestinian lawyers on the laws and procedures used in Israeli military courts; by increasing the prisoners' own knowledge of their rights; and by reviving grassroots human rights activism and volunteerism and working closely with community activists to increase their knowledge of civil and political rights from an international humanitarian law and international human rights perspective.

http://www.addameer.org/

Defence for Children International-Palestine Section (DCI-Palestine) is a national section of the international non-governmental child rights organization and movement, Defence for Children International (DCI), established in 1979.

DCI Palestine focuses on issues of:

Accountability: In appropriate cases DCI-Palestine submits complaints to the Israeli authorities on behalf of Palestinian children.

Child Detention: DCI each year monitors cases of approximately 500-700 Palestinian children (12-17 years) from the West Bank who are prosecuted in Israeli military courts after being arrested, interrogated and detained by the Israeli army, police or security agents.

DCI-Palestine has been documenting all *Palestinian child fatalities* at the hands of Israeli military and settler presence in the Occupied Palestinian Territories since the beginning of the second Intifada in September 2000.

Settlers who subscribe to *ultra-nationalistic* ideals and believe this land should be handed back to the Jewish people and are violent toward the Palestinian population, including children.

DCI regularly meets with relevant duty bearers and experts in the field of juvenile justice in order to identify weaknesses in the system, and to develop practical solutions to recruitment and use of *children in armed conflict* as prohibited under international law.

http://www.dci-palestine.org/.

New Profile is a group of feminist women and men, who are convinced that we need not live in a soldiers' state. Today, Israel is capable of a determined peace politics. It need not be a militarized society. We are convinced that we ourselves, our children, our partners, need not go on being endlessly mobilized; need not go on living as warriors.

New Profile realizes that the words "national security" have often masked calculated decisions to choose military action for the achievement of political goals. We are unwilling to take part in such choices. We will not go on enabling them by obediently, uncritically supplying soldiers to the military which implements them. We will not go on being recruited, raising children for recruitment, supporting recruited family members, while those in charge of the country go on easily deploying the army, rather than building other solutions.

Israeli law does not recognize the basic human right not to be a soldier. We regard the Israeli conscription law as discriminatory and non-democratic. For our part, we refuse to go on raising our children to see enlistment as a supreme and overriding value. We demand a fundamental change in the education system, so that it provides a truly democratic civic education, teaching the practice of peace and conflict resolution, rather than training children to enlist and accept warfare.

http://www.newprofile.org/english/about_en

Samidoun Palestinian Prisoner Solidarity Network is a network of organizers and activists, based in North America, working to build solidarity with Palestinian prisoners in their struggle for freedom. Samidoun developed out of the September-October 2011 hunger strike of Palestinian prisoners in Israeli jails, seeing a need for a dedicated network to support Palestinian prisoners. We work to raise awareness and provide resources about Palestinian political prisoners, their conditions, their demands, and their work for freedom for themselves, their fellow prisoners, and their homeland. We also work to organize campaigns to make political change and advocate for Palestinian prisoners' rights and freedoms.

Samidoun seeks to achieve justice for Palestinian prisoners through events, activities, resources, delegations, research and information-sharing, as well as building bridges with the prisoners' movement in Palestine. We seek to amplify the voices of Palestinian prisoners, former prisoners, prisoners' families, and Palestinian advocates for justice and human rights by translating, sharing and distributing news, interviews and materials from Palestine.

http://samidoun.ca/about-samidoun/

B'Tselem - The Israeli Information Center for Human Rights in the Occupied Territories was established in February 1989 by a group of prominent academics, attorneys, journalists, and Knesset members. It endeavors to document and educate the Israeli public and policymakers about human rights violations in the Occupied Territories, combat the phenomenon of denial prevalent among the Israeli public, and help create a human rights culture in Israel.

B'Tselem in Hebrew literally means "in the image of," and is also used as a synonym for human dignity. The word is taken from Genesis 1:27: "And God created humans in his image. In the image of God did He create him." It is in this spirit that the first article of the Universal Declaration of Human Rights states that "All human beings are born equal in dignity and rights."

As an Israeli human rights organization, B'Tselem acts primarily to change Israeli policy in the Occupied Territories and ensure that its government, which rules the Occupied Territories, protects the human rights of residents there and complies with its obligations under international law.

B'Tselem is independent and is funded by contributions from foundations in Europe and North America that support human rights activity worldwide, and by private individuals in Israel and abroad.

B'Tselem has attained a prominent place among human rights organizations. In December, 1989 it received the Carter-Menil Award for Human Rights. Its reports have gained B'Tselem a reputation for accuracy, and the Israeli authorities relate to them seriously. B'Tselem ensures the reliability of information it publishes by conducting its own fieldwork and research, the results of which are thoroughly cross-checked with relevant documents, official government sources, and information from other sources, among them Israeli, Palestinian, and other human rights organizations.
http://www.btselem.org/about_btselem

Breaking the Silence is an organization of veteran combatants who have served in the Israeli military since the start of the Second Intifada and have taken it upon themselves to expose the Israeli public to the reality of everyday life in the Occupied Territories. They endeavor to stimulate public debate about the price paid for a reality in which young soldiers face a civilian population on a daily basis, and are engaged in the control of that population's everyday life.

Soldiers who serve in the Territories witness and participate in military actions which change them immensely. Cases of abuse towards Palestinians, looting, and destruction of property have been the norm for years, but are still explained as extreme and unique cases. Our testimonies portray a different and much grimmer picture in which deterioration of moral standards finds expression in the character of orders and the rules of engagement, and are justified in the name of Israel's security. While this reality is known to Israeli soldiers and commanders, Israeli society continues to turn a blind eye, and to deny that what is done in its name. Discharged soldiers returning to civilian life discover the gap between the reality they encountered in the Territories, and the silence about this reality they encounter at home. In order to become civilians again, soldiers are forced to ignore what they have seen and done. Breaking the Silence strives to make heard the voices of these soldiers, pushing Israeli society to face the reality whose creation it has enabled.

Breaking the Silence collects and publishes testimonies from soldiers who, like us, have served in the West Bank, Gaza and East Jerusalem since September 2000, and holds lectures, house meetings, and other public events which bring to light the reality in the Territories through the voice of former combatants. We also conduct tours in Hebron and the South Hebron Hills region, with the aim of giving the Israeli public access to the reality which exists minutes from their own homes, yet is rarely portrayed in the media.

Founded in March 2004 by a group of soldiers who served in Hebron, Breaking the Silence has since acquired a special standing in the eyes of the Israeli public and in the media, as it is unique in giving voice to the experience of soldiers. To date, the organization has collected more than 700 testimonies from soldiers who represent all strata of Israeli society and cover nearly all units that operate in the Territories.

http://www.breakingthesilence.org.il/about/organization

Ahrar is a center for the study of prisoners and human rights that specializes in publishing violations of the Israeli occupation against the Palestinian prisoners in jails and monitoring the most prominent violations and offenses to the international customs, charters and regulations. It works on documenting, recording and publishing them in order to highlight on this group of people that are suffering.

The center also monitors, records and follows up the other violations inside the occupied territories including extra judicial killing, stealing lands, demolitions of homes and maltreatment of debtors. It seeks to publish freedoms and enhance the concepts of human rights in the Palestinian occupied territories, to build it and to enhance its position inside the Palestinian community in accordance with its vision which is derived from the universal declaration of human rights and international agreements based in this vision.

Ahrar supports Palestinian prisoners through the publication of violations they suffer in the occupation jails and activation of their issue in the media, raises issues over the occupation, some of the abuses carried out against our prisoners exploiting the Israeli Supreme Courts, and works on the support of the prisoners in all ways so they do not feel alone in this battle with the occupier. Ahrar has issued reports naming affected by prison authorities and conditions.

http://ahrar.ps/en/

The Palestine Israel Ecumenical Forum (PIEF), a Programme of the World Council of Churches and established in 2007, is an instrument to "catalyze and coordinate new and existing church advocacy for peace, aimed at ending the illegal occupation of Palestine in accordance with UN resolutions, and demonstrating its commitment to inter-religious action for peace and justice that serves all the peoples of the region."

The scope of the PIEF is worldwide because the crisis in the Middle East and its solutions are increasingly global in scope.

The PIEF works toward increasing solidarity between and among churches committed to peace and justice for communities living under occupation. Its inter-faith dimension invites people of other religions in the Middle East and elsewhere to join the search and struggle for a just and comprehensive peace.

The core actions of PIEF will address:
- Actions challenging government support for the occupation
- Actions challenging public support for the occupation
- Actions challenging theological and biblical justifications for the occupation and
- Actions maintaining viable the Palestinian Christian presence in the Holy Land.